Advance Praise

This book authored by Belen Loreto Grand successfully straddles the two cultures in which Filipino nurse immigrants and OFWs live, cultures that at times conflict and collide around the issue of sending money to their families back home. The collectivistic culture of the Philippines values the economic and social well-being of the family, often to the subservience of the individual member's need, whereas the individualistic culture of the US prioritizes self-reliance and financial independence over family need. The author deftly interweaves elements of both cultural contexts to enable readers to understand the push and pull that many Filipino nurses and OFWs experience. The book renders the individual stories, some of which are the author's own, with thoughtfulness, empathy, and compassion, while simultaneously provides guidance to those affected with doses of much-needed objectivity and pragmatism. It is a good read and contains valuable self-help!

DIVINA GROSSMAN, PhD, RN, FAAN

President, University of St. Augustine for Health Sciences, San Marcos, California. Former Chancellor, University of Massachusetts Dartmouth. Dartmouth, MA, USA

Managing your finances can seem like endless frustration for many of us. Layer on top of that cultural and familial expectations, and it can feel like you'll never get ahead or make anyone happy. In "Family Matters", Belen Loreto Grand lovingly tackles the intricacies of the financial dynamics many overseas Filipino workers face, from learning how to set boundaries to changing the conversation around familial expectations, all while maintaining respect for the culture of gifting and reciprocity. Belen has given readers a fantastic resource for re-framing what, for many, is a source of great stress and anxiety. This book is for anyone struggling to find balance between their new reality in a foreign country and maintaining close ties to loved ones in a way that doesn't break the bank.

LIZ LAJOIE, author of *From Zero to Zen.*
The Coaches' CFO

The book is very educational and it can help not only Filipino nurses and OFWs but anyone who wants to be financially empowered. The acronym FORGIVE as a tool for changing one's perspective is very powerful. To forgive is one of the hardest things to do. Following the strategies outlined in the acronym will be helpful in knowing oneself. As written in the Scriptures "Know Thyself".

This book is value-laden, especially of long-lasting Filipino values which made it more interesting. The phenomenon of helping others, as the author had discussed is cultural among Filipinos which I can personally relate as I assisted in the education of members of my family and who are grateful for my assistance. This book reminded me of these words from the Bible "To whom much is given, much is required"; an admonition ingrained in us by our Dean at Silliman University College of Nursing and served and still serve as our guide to serve people and our country all for the glory of God!

DR. GLENDA S. ARQUIZA, Chairperson, Professional Regulatory Board of Nursing.Professional Regulation Commission. Republic of the Philippines

Belen Loreto Grand's book is reflective of what some of the Filipino nurses and OFWs have experienced working abroad. Some are able to overcome the family-money drama that happens in many families but others are tied to the same problem forever. I commend the author for writing a picturesque description of our country.

LYDIA A. PALAYPAY, Former Dean, Institute of Nursing, Far Easter University, Manila, Philippines

If you are a Filipino nurse or overseas Filipino worker, you will be empowered to make the right financial decision with your families back in your country. Overwhelmed by balancing the financial challenges of a new country and at the same time helping families economically back home? Here are the tools and strategies how to assist families, maintain harmony and avoid the family money drama that often comes into play with a win-win situation for all involved.

NORMAN PLOTKIN, Certified Hypnotherapist, author of *Take Charge of Your Cancer*

It is a well written book and to the point. There are a lot of tips as to how to be entertained without paying so much for entertainment. How we are all tied to our own culture that sometimes it's hard to say no for fear of being ostracized. Everything she wrote in the book has somehow touched anybody who is an immigrant. I salute the author, for being such a brave soul, for baring her soul to the reader.

RAQUEL CANCIO, BSN, RN, Miltown, New Jersey

A very powerful and relevant book. Most overseas Filipino workers (OFWs) would likely be able to relate to this and hopefully they would be able to deal with situations when there are times they need to say "NO" to unending financial requests.

LVM QUIRIMIT, MSN, RN, Clinical Instructor, School of Nursing. College of Health Professions. Armstrong State University. Savannah, Georgia. Author of *Hamon Ng Buhay OFW*

Family Matters brings light to what can often be a very dark subject. Money in general can shut down and destroy so many relationships. I found this book to be very helpful bringing the conversation about money in a way that is constructive instead of destructive. Bravo!

LEAH BRAMHAM CARVER, Spa Wellness Coach and Yoga Teacher. Jupiter, Florida. Author of *Undoing Hashimotos*

The book is very useful especially to all Filipino nurses and OFW's. I have not seen anybody write about such a delicate topic amongst Filipinos and I am sure a lot of people can relate to the subject. Great read, very well explained and easy to understand.

GERARDO ESCANDOR, BSN.
Sicklerville, New Jersey

The author did an amazing job with this topic of money and family! This book is relatable to any person, not just Filipino families who help family members out. A lot of this information is what I could relate to as a person who did not have much, but later acquired more than others around so they depended on me. This caused issues and friction in our relationships. I am relating to her words. Thanks for sharing this message with the world.

NIKKI C. PATTERSON, Certified educator,
entrepreneur, educational consultant,
author of *How To Win As A Principal*

This book presents different approaches types and forms of assistance that lead to an improved life to both the provider and the receiver. These stories lead to a realization that the givers also encounter other types and forms of difficulties just as the receivers.

LORNA GABITO, Former Statistician IV. Head,
Fruit crops, Vegetables and Root Crops Statistics Section.
Crops Statistics Division of the Philippine Statistics
Authority. Manila, Philippines

Family Matters

Family Matters

*Making the Right Financial
Decision for Your Filipino Family*

BELEN LORETO GRAND

NEW YORK

LONDON • NASHVILLE • MELBOURNE • VANCOUVER

Family Matters

Making the Right Financial Decision for Your Filipino Family

Published in New York, New York, by Morgan James Publishing in partnership with Difference Press. Morgan James is a trademark of Morgan James, LLC. www.MorganJamesPublishing.com

The Morgan James Speakers Group can bring authors to your live event. For more information or to book an event visit The Morgan James Speakers Group at www.TheMorganJamesSpeakersGroup.com.

ISBN 9781683509547 paperback
ISBN 9781683509554 eBook
Library of Congress Control Number: 2018901075

Cover Design by:
Rachel Lopez
www.r2cdesign.com

Interior Design by:
Chris Treccani
www.3dogcreative.net

In an effort to support local communities, raise awareness and funds, Morgan James Publishing donates a percentage of all book sales for the life of each book to Habitat for Humanity Peninsula and Greater Williamsburg.

Get involved today! Visit
www.MorganJamesBuilds.com

To my husband Robert, for all the love and support you have given me through all the years.

In memory of my mother, Enriqueta Santa Iglesia Loreto (RIP), who gave so much and empowered many to be financially independent. You're the best, Mom!

Table of Contents

Introduction

When can I stop giving financial assistance to my family back in the Philippines?

I bet that like most Filipino nurses, you have been sending money to your family for various reasons for the past decade or more and have agonized over whether you can ever stop, or if that's even the right thing to do.

Have you ever dreamed of the day when you can break free of feeling like you have to help your relatives financially? Maybe you've wondered if your family will ever be monetarily independent. Maybe you've hoped they'll magically become entrepreneurs and start living their lives to the fullest. How great would it be to go home for vacation and share the expenses with your other family members equally, instead of being the only person paying for everyone's good time?

The truth is, most of us want to help. It's deeply ingrained in our culture. Filipino nurses have unsurpassed kindness, and sincerely want to provide equal economic opportunities to our families back home. As healthcare professionals, we are world-renowned for our compassion, warmth, and generosity. Most of us are truly kind-hearted and courageous.

Thousands of us endured the typical immigrant rites of passage in a new country. Some of you left your babies or young children and husbands behind, at least initially, when you first came to the land of Uncle Sam. I can imagine the tears you shed when you said your goodbyes at the airport and the many personal sacrifices you went through to earn those coveted green bucks.

I know, because my colleagues and I have our own story of scavenging the dumpster at midnight in search of mattresses, television sets, and wooden tables when we first arrived in this land of opportunity. We walked two miles in Florida's blazing summer heat to do our grocery shopping at a cheaper store, and save our dollars for our family. We endured crying spells when we missed our loved ones back home. Our path was not covered with scented roses; we had to adjust to challenges like language barriers, culture shock, and miscommunications such as the embarrassment of misusing the gender pronouns *he/she* (something I still do often, confusing my husband, LOL).

Giving financial assistance to family members is a noble act. It feels good when you are invited to be the guest of honor for a niece or nephew's college graduation (especially if he/she graduated with honors!). I can imagine your face as you sit there, an aunt or uncle beaming with pride. Or how about the way your heart jumps for joy when you can play the heroine and financially rescue a family member from the abyss of mounting hospital bills that you know they just can't afford to pay no matter how many jobs they hold back in the Philippines? You may save your family member from having to use his house as a collateral to pay the medical bills.

Why is it that some extended Filipino families seem to have great relationships where they all pitch in financially during family parties, and yet others struggle, rarely even getting a sincere "thank you" from a family member for the gifts given to them? Many Filipino nurses like you are hounded by the feeling of being *personally responsible* for everyone in the family back in the country. Some of us have very needy relatives and we struggle to navigate this family money drama; others seem to be able to breeze through with ease and fluidity, seemingly without feeling the financial burden on their shoulders. Those who struggle are so agitated that, unbeknownst to them, they are vulnerable to stress-related afflictions like breast cancer, hypertension, or other health crises. Wouldn't you like to have the secret sauce these nurses seem to possess, the ones who know how to set firm boundaries or when to say enough is enough when it comes to financial assistance—and *not* feel an ounce of guilt?

You're about to discover the not-so-secret path to a life of joy and abundance with the information this book will provide you. *The fact that you are reading this book means that you are destined to hear my message.* This is a pivotal period in your life. You may have been contemplating how to make the right financial decisions for your family back home, but are paralyzed with the *feeling of guilt of abandoning your family or fear of being ostracized.* But the thought keeps reverberating, *"Is there ever a good time to stop the financial largess to my family?"* Or, *"How can I avoid the drama if I stop giving money to my family?"*

Most financial books and magazines focus on the many aspects of making or saving money. Some delve further into how to invest your hard-earned income using mutual funds, IRAs, or other investment vehicles. Others discuss the ins and outs of what types of insurance to purchase, differentiating *term* from *life* insurance, providing details of the importance of disability, or long-term insurance, or revocable trusts, and other financial intricacies. For those who are interested in stocks and options, there are many resources. However, the book in your hand doesn't quite fit the mold mentioned above.

Have you ever seen personal finance guru Suze Orman on public television, or read any of the series of books she has written regarding money and personal wealth?[1] If you haven't, I highly recommend getting a couple of copies, one to keep and one to give as a gift to a family member. Her book *9 Steps to Financial Freedom* was the first finance book I read here in America, and it contained a lot of pearls of wisdom for us to take note of. She has been invited to speak in the Philippines twice, and I agree with her observations regarding our money culture that "Filipinos struggle to say *no* to family members." She advises that we only give money for our families' needs, not for luxuries. Her accolades about our love of family and our beautiful Filipino culture are flattering and true, but I am also in agreement with her that our habits of offering too much hospitality and living beyond our means need changing. If we want to improve and stabilize our family finances, we need to modify some of our customs and traditions. *We need to help our family members become better managers of their finances.*

Many cultures encounter financial challenges, but ours in particular is profound and a bit complicated. There is so much to decipher and analyze, and to most people, it is easier to continue the status quo rather than ruffle the feathers of family members or confront them head-on. The discussion of money is taboo; many of us would rather continue working a few extra shifts because it could open emotional wounds if we bring up the *family-money drama.* It is difficult for us to assert ourselves (myself included, it is cultural!), set limits, and be honest with our families. We tend to rationalize and hope that soon, we will be relieved of this financial responsibility that we took on voluntarily (or maybe involuntarily). We have mastered the art of wearing the happy mask for our loved ones, even if we are hurting deep inside us.

Filipino nurses often work double shifts, and when they're in their twenties or thirties, it may not feel like a big deal. But wait until you reach mid-forties like most of my clients—that is when you feel the aching back and tired feet. The extra cash gained by putting in a 60- to 80-hour workweek no longer brings excitement. One of my clients, Liz, used to put in 20 to 30 hours of overtime every week for months before she went home to the Philippines, so she could fill up 15 *balikbayan* (returnee) boxes with television sets, microwave ovens, stereo systems, computers, cameras, Oil of Olay creams, soaps, and chocolates galore. If she could have bought out all of Costco or Walmart, she would have. That's how much she wanted to share her bounty with her family.

It took me years to figure out ways to be at the top, professionally and financially. Like some Filipino nurses, you may have been a trailblazer yourself in your field of expertise. I was one of the first graduates from an ARNP (Advanced Registered Nurse Practitioner) Program at Florida International University, one of the first Filipinos to become a critical care registered nurse (CCRN) in the 1980s, and the first Filipino to be a liver and GI transplant coordinator at Jackson Health System. One of my proudest moments was being instrumental in opening the Center for Liver Diseases at the University of Miami, where I became the Research Administrator for the department later on. Of course, my salary was ample, and I didn't mind helping many members of our family and educated my brothers, nephews, nieces—even cousins from different generations, since I, too, believed in higher education as a passport to financial stability.

The knowledge I share with you in this book took me several years to learn and refine, so reading this once may not make you an instant millionaire. Although it depends! Probably your vessels are so open that you can win the $100 million lottery. With just a bit of tweaking of your mindset, you could instantly attract abundance that could turn your life around 360 degrees.

But, I want to remind you that it is a pre-requisite that you put in the *willingness, time, and sustained effort* to change the dynamics of how to live your life so that you manifest joy and abundance. This book is the start. The many "aha" moments and the tools and strategies outlined in this book will guide you *not only to financial prosperity but to peace, love and joy in your life.*

As you read through the following chapters, I highly recommend using a journal to jot down your progress so you can monitor any improvements or tweak what is not working. The act of writing makes a big difference. Reading and practicing the strategies outlined here could be a pivotal moment in your life. Maybe you have been hosting relatives for over a month now who need time to acclimatize to the American way of life, and your home situation is getting a bit sticky. How's the bathroom traffic in your house? Are you the proverbial Uber chauffeur for their appointments? Are your teenage boys getting along with the guests? Is your food budget ballooning? In this book, you'll find strategies on self-care to save your sanity.

Oh and wait, don't let me forget to mention the many *lies and fears* that you have downloaded into your money belief system. Nurses are familiar with psychotherapy or seeing a shrink for emotional instability when stuff unravels in our lives, and yet all too often we don't clean up old baggage learned by cultural osmosis that affects our manifestation of wealth and abundance.

Duh ... what does this mean? I can hear your whispers! In a study published in 2013 by *Nature Neuroscience*, researchers trained mice to fear the smell of cherry blossoms. Then Brian Dias and Kerry Ressler at the Emory University School of Medicine looked at what was happening inside mice's sperm, where they found that a section of DNA responsible for the adverse reaction to the scent of cherry blossoms scent was more active.[2] Not only were the mice's direct offspring "extremely sensitive" to cherry blossoms, the next generation would avoid the scent as well, despite never having experienced it before in their lives. Both generations also showed changes in brain structure. The report concluded that "the experiences of a parent, even before conceiving, markedly influence both structure and function in the nervous system of subsequent generations." Neuroscientists have recently focused on how our past beliefs or childhood experiences are affecting us emotionally, and why they could be the limiting blocks to our wealth manifestation.

I urge you *not* to put this book down until you have updated the files in your brain and downloaded the tools and strategies outlined here. Before we move on to the first chapter, take a moment to close your eyes and imagine how your life will be two years from now if you have unlimited financial abundance and are living a joyful life. I don't know what the definition of that is to you. It could be a net income of $20,000 per month or $50,000 passive income from your stock investments and dividends. Focus on your feelings of euphoria over not having to worry about finances. You are so relaxed, you are getting a weekly massage, taking exotic trips with your family regularly. Sending $500 per month via Xoom.com to your family in the Philippines is not draining your pocketbook anymore, and you are filled with gratitude. Everyone is happy; in fact you feel so benevolent that you are planning to fund college scholarships to the children of your high school classmates. Maybe you want to rebuild the church that badly needed repairs in your city. *Expand your mind even further and allow yourself the opportunity to bring out the best in you, what contributions do you think you can do to repair this world?* Better yet, the planned family reunion in the Philippines is just months away, and you are full of excitement about diving in the crystal blue-green waters and basking at the white sand beaches of Palawan island where even Microsoft's Bill Gates reportedly purchased a private island to have lots of fun and sun.

You can resolve this financial conundrum you find yourself in—and you can be a catalyst for change in the century-old dilemma we Filipinos find ourselves in about family and money. We all have to put in sincere effort, we nurses and OFWs and loved ones left in the Philippines. This book will explore your fastest, easiest path to solve the Rubik's cube of Philippine society's cultural issues—and your issues—with money and family. You will be empowered to take the necessary leap, and move forward in financial freedom and joy.

> "*When you care deeply about someone or something, repairs are worth your investment of time, energy, effort, heart and resources. Whether it is to repair a broken trust or a damaged relationship, take the initiative to make it right and make it better.*"
> SUSAN C. YOUNG

Chapter 1

MY STORY

A score and fifteen years ago, I left the Philippines with four other nurses, all of us full of enthusiasm and ambition, sure that this great country we fondly call the USA would fulfill our hopes and dreams. My beloved mother bade me farewell with all her smiles, yet deep inside, I sensed a sadness in her. She had a hunch … and a year after my arrival in Miami, she died of congestive heart failure. My beloved mom, the one who instilled in me my love of travel, left me with many unfulfilled dreams of trips together. I was not able to experience the grand cafes of Vienna with her, stroll with her alongside the old canals of Venice, nor be in awe of Mona Lisa at the Louvre in Paris together.

I had initially planned to serve in my province of Leyte (famously known as Imelda Marcos' birthplace, also where super typhoon Haiyan unleashed its wrath on Philippine soil);

I dreamed of empowering the people of my town whose poverty I witnessed every day. The gap between rich and poor was widening as the years went by. So, after graduation from nursing school at Far Eastern University in Manila in 1980, I decided to volunteer and work as a rural health nurse. Still, my mother had insisted: "Go to America, the land of opportunities. If you don't like it there, you can always come back after one year, but at least try while you're still young." I sensed my mother's urgency, so I followed her advice.

I embarked on this epic journey with vigor and determination at the tender age of 23. My friends and I had a *naivete'* that somehow shielded us from the realities of living and working in America. We couldn't contain our excitement—in fact, our eagerness to accept a dinner invitation from our colleague's aunt during a layover in San Francisco made us miss our connecting flight to Miami, but it didn't perturb us. No problem: we excitedly took pictures to document our arrival outside the airport. "Sir, are we in California?" we asked the security officer, who responded, "Yes ma'am, we're in San Francisco, California." We had no clue that San Francisco was part of California—this was before Google and GPS!

I called my brother in L.A. to pick us up at the San Francisco airport and he said wryly, "Do you know that you're about a five- to six-hour drive from Los Angeles?" Huh! I didn't know. Oh boy! We giggled, waited for the next flight, and slept at the airport; no worries at all. Neither did we have plans for where we were going to live upon arrival in Florida, just the name of our employer hospital. We didn't even have anybody to pick us up at the airport. Sometimes, innocence is a virtue indeed. At dawn, I reluctantly bought hot chocolate and broke the $100 bill my oldest brother had kindly sent me. I bought a cup each for my colleagues, but we couldn't get any liquid to come out of the straw. We took more straws until finally the proprietor said, "That's not a straw, but a stirrer. You have to drink it directly from the cup." I'd never used a stirrer for hot chocolate or, for that matter, ever ordered one—I had never been able to afford one! Upon arrival in Florida, we were surprised when a group of Filipino nurses picked us up at the airport and hosted us for a few days in their apartments, a true *bayanihan spirit (Filipino custom derived from the word 'bayan,' which means town or community. The term refers to the spirit of communal unity, work and cooperation to achieve a particular goal)* Welcome to America!

Like most Filipino overseas workers, or OFW, our passports were stamped prior to departure. We found our first mattress in a trash bin and snuck it into our apartment at midnight to avoid embarrassment if seen by our neighbors; our first black and white television set, tables, and chairs were all scavenged the same way. Our torn bedsheets were donated by the hospital, and we recycled the plastic spoons and forks we had used at work and took them home to reuse before we purchased our set of cutlery. We walked a few miles in the August Florida heat to do our grocery shopping since we wanted to spare the few dollars for our cab ride back to our apartments. Uber wasn't around yet, and even if it had been, we would have been too stingy to take advantage of it. We calculated our expenses down to the last few cents.

We also had many embarrassing moments, one of which was when we ordered pizza, we were too bashful to ask what the server meant when he asked 'whole or slice' we ordered 'whole' since we understood that word, we truly didn't understand what 'slice' meant. When our order was ready, we were surprised to receive large whole pizza for each of us. We just laughed and brought the leftovers to our roommates.

My sister Anne, who left for Austria in 1975 to work as a registered nurse, and my oldest brother, Adrian, were major contributors to achieving my mother's dream of a college education for all her children. G-d knows, they have their own chapters to write of the hardships and challenges as new immigrants. I shiver just imagining the harsh, cold winters of Colorado, where my brother first came to join his fiancée in 1976. And as for my sister's escapades in Europe, even the thought of mastering the German language makes my tongue twist!! My sister had her personal life on hold, I perceived that the burden of educating her younger siblings was placed early on her shoulders, a typical practice of families in the Philippines and one that is still rampant today.

The guilt of not helping one's family overpowers many immigrants. Marriages are even postponed until one has educated a younger sibling or two. I contributed my fair share within a month after arriving in August, 1982, and sent my regular monthly remittance to finance a younger brother who was finishing his veterinary medical education as well as helped produce more nurses, a geologist, and other professionals in our extended family. Oh, by the way, I helped settle some of them in America, too, and shared my wisdom and guidance in their job search. Today, all are financially independent, happily living their lives.

To those left behind in the Philippines, immigrants to America seem very lucky. Are we? Yes, considering that millions of people would love to reach the shores of this great country to put their talents and ambitions toward the pursuit of economic prosperity and go after their much-clichéd American dream. Many have risked their lives, swum in shark-infested waters, been smuggled overseas, and met other catastrophes just for the opportunity to work and live here. Getting a valid work visa isn't an option for everyone; only those who qualify are allowed to work here. I know illegal immigrants, many of whom are Filipinos, are a real issue, but for the sake of this book, we will defer from that discussion.

Most of you endured the homesickness of anything Filipino: food, lavish fiestas to honor patron saints of a city or town, the camaraderie of friends, memories with loving family, and so much more. But, you remember that a hundred US dollars set aside for your family will bring them much prosperity. Considering that the exchange rate is currently 49 Philippine pesos for each US dollar and, according to the Philippine Statistics Authority, the average 2016 annual income of Filipino families was approximately PHP 267,000, it's easy to see why even a small US dollar amount is welcomed by any Filipino family.

Not every Filipino jumps at the chance to immigrate. My mother passed up her chance; she was already married with children when an uncle, then a colonel in the US Navy, gave her a chance to immigrate to America. She chose love and family, a noble thing to do, but she was not without regret, which is why she didn't want me to squander my golden chance. As one of the few agronomists from the prestigious University of the

Philippines in the 1950s, my father declined an offer to be a soil analyst for a pineapple plantation in Hawaii, but as my mother often said, "Belen, you would have not been born!" Then again, who knows? Maybe I would have been a citizen through *jus soli*, born in the USA!

It has been 34 years since my beloved mother passed away on July 4, 1983. As a nurse, I carried the guilt and regret of not having rendered excellent care and compassion to her when she became ill, but thankfully my aunt and mother's confidante, who was the former chief nurse of the Armed Forces of the Philippines, was at her bedside. She reassured me and my sister that my mother died peacefully, proud and happy that she accomplished her task of ensuring that we all got a college education. She apparently mentioned our names, all eight of us professionals. Five were working abroad, one was a major in the Philippine navy, and two were awaiting visas to immigrate to America. She was hopeful that we would improve our economic lot and not fritter away our talents in our native country so that we can continue to help each other.

I was so optimistic then that an economic miracle would occur in our country, dubbed the *Pearl of the* Orient, but will it happen? That was the big question. The brain-drain continued for several years due to political and other socio-economic circumstances. Education of the masses was one of the solutions, as my mother had emphasized.

Economic prosperity is clearly on the horizon. The remittance of OFWs as one of the main engines of the Philippine economy reached a record high of 26.9 billion US dollars in 2016.[3] But behind the façade of happy families getting together and eating at Chow King, shopping at SM malls, hosting *balikbayans* or enjoying the white sand beaches, there are many untold stories of heartache, family drama, and trauma that are buried deep in the psyche just for the sake of *pakikisama* (getting along) and helping each other. And all that stress takes its toll. It's not uncommon for Filipino nurses in America to be diagnosed with breast cancer in their 40s or 50s (I know some of them personally), and other ailments like strokes, hypertension, cardiac conditions and other signs of stress are, sadly, breaking families apart.

Many are cognizant of the *family-money dilemma*. When the financial crisis hit America, I felt like a bullet train hit me right on its tracks. I realized that despite my more than 25 years of sharing my bounty, someone, somehow, was always going to need to be rescued monetarily. As the saying goes, when it rained, it really poured, and our own finances were in trouble after I left my lucrative career as an ARNP due to stress at work and helped managed my husband's business, which encountered rough spots just like most businesses in America during the great recession.

We lived frugally to ensure we could still live a joyful, simple life, and economized by watching inexpensive or free symphonies. These simple pleasures rapidly became the talk of my extended family back home, and the green-eyed monster of jealousy seemed to be spreading the news to everyone that we lived a very grand life. Nobody listened to our explanations when we had to set limits on our financial assistance; my complaints about the expense of private medical insurance fell on deaf ears. My family demanded I help educate a brother's grandchild.

When I quietly protested, I was treated like a pariah, an outcast from my own tribe.

I had to do some soul-searching, and made it my mission to dig deep to try to understand the rationale and possible solutions to this common quandary. As I talked to other Filipino nurses, it dawned on me that this vicious cycle of financial co-dependency is a common occurrence that many have endured. Some told me that it caused family break-ups, but many are accepting this predicament as the status quo with a sigh and "What can you do?"

If this sounds like you and your family, I can imagine the years of deep-seated anger and dissatisfaction you have likely harbored. Despite your attempts to set limits to the amount of money you send, your family is probably incredulous and don't understand why you can't continue to provide financial largess. Our families in the Philippines don't seem to understand America's own financial crises. Many of us feel we can't even talk about our own financial difficulties for fear of being ostracized or causing family disputes.

I've been there, and have made many mistakes in dealing with family-money issues, hence my quest to share with you the tools I learned to effectively navigate these treacherous waters. There are simple, profound and effective ways to deal with this predicament. Of course, we don't want to abandon our famous trait of warm hospitality and love of family, but we need to change, modify, and rethink the dynamics of money culture and our outlook about finances to stop the leakage of anger, guilt, resentment, and misunderstanding and so that love will continue to flourish among Filipino families.

Chapter 2

LOVE OF FAMILY VS. LOVE OF MONEY

"It's more fun in the Philippines!"

That ubiquitous tourism ad shown on every airline and super ferry is so compelling that my client Beth can't help but smile and hum along with the song—in fact, she's teary-eyed. She is a registered nurse who left her country 21 years ago. Her last visit was in 2007, so she is ecstatic at the prospect of seeing her loved ones and showing her children that life in the Philippines is really more fun, just as the advertisement says it is. The picturesque landscapes of Baguio's famous Rice Terraces, considered one of the natural wonders of the world, and the clear aquamarine water, limestone cliffs, and lagoons of Palawan, which *Conde Nast Travel* readers voted the second most beautiful island in the world in 2016, flash on her television screen while watching the Filipino channels. The sun and fun, frolicking teenagers diving in the newly discovered caves of Samar Island, and the sparkling white sand beaches are shown everywhere.

She's thinking of taking her extended family to the small island called *Kalanggaman* off Leyte, which is about two hours from her province of Cebu. She's heard the boat rides and prices are still affordable, since most tourists haven't yet invaded this island paradise of a bird sanctuary with its sparkling crystal-clear water and pink and white sand beaches. So unlike Palawan, where millionaires have bought some of the islands already. It's been shown on the Travel Channel so often, it's no wonder the place is now unaffordable for most Filipinos unless the family has a financier from abroad.

Her nostalgia of that time her family gathered together 10 years ago is so overwhelming. She misses the lavish feasts at their house where all her nephews and nieces, would come in quietly, bashfully asking a blessing as they politely took her hand and pressed their small hands to their foreheads as a sign of respect. Sometimes, she wonders, "Why did I leave my country to work so hard in America?"

The loud chants of *"Viva Pit Senor"* by the devotees of the *Sinulog,* or *Santo Nino Festival,* an annual cultural and religious festival held on the third Sunday of January, is now reverberating in her ears. It is the grandest and most colorful festival in the Philippines, with street dancing that competes with the *Calle Ocho Festival* in Miami. It is the most celebrated in her province; she forgoes her Christmas vacation so she can attend this historic event that commemorates the landing of the

Portuguese explorer Fernando de Magellan in Cebu city when he claimed the area in April, 1521 in the name of King Philip of Spain. The *Santo Nino* wooden statue, a holy child image of Jesus, was his gift to Rajah Humabon's wife, Hana Amihan, as a baptismal present.[4]

The ninth day of the festival culminates in the *Sinulog*, or Grand Parade, with a Pontifical Mass by the Cardinal. Devotees gather to obtain blessings for those who are in poor health or have dire problems to overcome and who need the intervention of the *Santo Nino*. Beth thinks about her own family-money dilemma, but she tries to shrug it off. The *Santo Nino* devotion is a very important part of most Filipinos' religious life. For spectators on the streets, it is a scene to behold, and for the participants who are street dancing, it is a way to show their utmost devotion to G-d. This gathering is also a grand family reunion time, after all, what is money for without a loving family? That's her reason and for many Filipino nurses, the *raison d' être* for working double shifts, exploring the foreign lands of Japan, or sweating it out in the middle east. Everyone comes back home for this much-awaited feast of the patron saint of a city or town. Beth and her friends will reminisce over old memories and make new experiences together with loved ones. The old generation will be introduced to the younger generation.

Food, oh ... the Filipino delicacies and exotic fruits! The street food of *turon*, ripe banana in crisp egg roll wrappers with strips of exotic jackfruit inside fried to perfection, the crunchy pastry, o*tap*, the sweet and succulent mangoes, and the variety of fish dishes. The fresh vegetables at the produce market, where you can also chat with vendors who make a homemade, pure, thick chocolate mixture that they put on top of their rice *puto(steamed rice cake served as a snack)*—how can Beth forget the tastes of her native country? Of course, she will be designated to purchase the star of any Filipino feast: the *pork lechon*. She isn't sure what that will cost, but she willingly says that it will be fine, since that is her way of sharing her bounty with her family.

Beth is vacillating between being excited at the prospect of seeing her family and worrying about her finances. She's very anxious about the expenses she will incur during this three-week vacation. How about the *pasalubon*g (gift or souvenir)? This is a tradition that she can't ignore; she has to bring the much-awaited homecoming gifts. This is imprinted in the Filipino culture, which entails a certain sense of camaraderie, or *pakikisama,* among family and friends. She deems it necessary as a *balikbayan* to bring friends and family something back, almost as an effort toward maintaining her good graces. She worries what her friends and family will think of her if she doesn't bring back anything for them—of course, they won't just settle with something inexpensive, they want brand names, a pair of Ray-Ban sunglasses or a Kate Spade clutch. Some distant relatives hopefully will settle with chocolates, lipstick, soaps, or cleansing creams.

Beth has barely six months to prepare for this much-awaited trip, and although she is very excited, there's a gnawing feeling in her stomach. The overtime shifts she had requested were not granted. It is summertime, and snowbirds are scarce. She was hoping to get at least a 12-hour shift per week to pay for her expenses, no matter how back-breaking it is to be working now that she is in her mid-forties and she has less energy, but she assures herself that the excitement at the prospect of being with family and friends in a few months will keep her going.

She's also hoping that her brother, who is a physician in Cebu, will help with some of the expenses—after all, she helped send him to medical school and she's still helping with the private education of his children. They have a four-bedroom, three-bath house,; Beth just needs to convince her teenage boys to stay with their younger cousins. "Hopefully," she thinks, "they all will get along and just have fun."

Beth is fully aware that she needs to save more money for this trip so they can all have the much-anticipated fun and sun vacation; she knows the burden is on her shoulders to pay for everyone in the family. She has been surfing the Internet for decent airfares. The sound of Donna Summer's *She Works Hard for the Money* is getting louder and louder, until she finds a good deal that will save her hundreds of dollars, even though they have to stay over for eight hours in Dubai. She books the flight. Oh, my—the airfare alone is costing her almost $6000 dollars for five of them, how much overtime work will she need? Beth laughs at herself: her iPhone's Siri seems to have anticipated her thoughts. *Recalculate!*

Beth is hit with the reality of the mounting expenses she is about to face for her upcoming vacation. She thinks of her colleague Eva, also one of my clients, who recently went back to the Philippines and forewent the *pasalubong*. Instead, Eva treated her close family and friends to dinner out at a hamburger chain called Jollibee that didn't cost her an arm and a leg. But

Beth ponders: Hmmm, Eva was criticized and ostracized by her family and is labeled as *tihik* (a Cebuano dialect word for stingy, or *barat* in Tagalog). Eva warned Beth not to follow in her footsteps, because now Eva's relatives have almost disowned her. Apparently the neighbors are now taunting Eva's mom that she did not properly educate her daughter: "*Eva is such a miser, doesn't know how to share G-d's gifts, was not given the proper discipline, no wonder she is having difficulty in America.*" The whole town is gossiping about Eva's "antisocial" behavior. Eva lamented: "They don't seem to understand that I have to save money for my son's college education. I went home to see them, but their expectations were different. I thought they loved me, but it seems like they *loved my money*. Now, I don't even feel like talking to them, nor do I want to be around them. My children are very upset and it's causing a family rift, after all those years of helping them. When is enough ever enough?"

Beth is grateful that her son has a scholarship at a prestigious private school, at Ransom Everglades of all places, where the children of diplomats and elites study. But in two years, he will be attending college, and a strict family budget will have to be observed since his older son's dream universities of Harvard and Stanford have steep price tags. Beth is hoping her daughter Sarah, who at 12 is very athletic and currently attends a public elementary school, will get a scholarship at a private high school since she is also a tennis ace. Her youngest, Joseph, age 10, aims to be the next Filipino Joshua Bell. With his talent on violin, he has represented his class in different county and state competitions. The lessons cost Beth a hefty sum of money every month, but pulling him out would be devastating for him. She rationalizes that the violin lessons will hone Joseph's skills and garner him a college scholarship to the prestigious Juilliard School of Music in New York.

For now, Beth is trying to forgo the idea of saving until after the family vacation. Even if she has to max out her credit cards, she will do what she thinks is appropriate to show her love and care for her family back home.

Culturally Ingrained Co-Dependency

Another client, Liz, has difficulty setting boundaries with her younger sister when she asked for financial assistance. Liz's sister wants her to continue paying for their new Honda Odyssey for another year. Liz confides that her sister has a socialite mentality, maintaining a gym membership at the nearby hotel and spa where her college friends, who are married to some of the techies in Cebu, start their day after dropping off their kids at school. Liz's last conversation with her sister about financial planning and the need to stop trying to keep up with the Joneses fell on deaf ears. Her sister still shops a lot at SM mall for her Louis Vuitton bags and Ferragamo shoes; her passion for venti latte has not subsided. With her husband away in London working as a nurse, her sister confided, the sky-level Starbucks at the mall relieves her from the loneliness of not having her spouse around. There seems to be no way of getting around her sister's ingrained co-dependency. Liz can only pray that her sister will stop the luxuries that she can't afford if she wants to save enough for her children's education. Liz sister's response is always "*bahala na,*" or similar to *"come what may"* or *"que sera, sera"*: a fatalistic or laid back phrase widely used in the

Philippines and that makes Liz feel annoyed. Her sister, despite being a nurse herself, just laughs and teases Liz that "living in America has made you a worrier, you should leave it up to G-d. If He takes care of the bees and the flowers, He will take care of my family."

More *Pasalubong*, Please

Beth has been revising her vacation budget due to the all too familiar tradition of *pasalubong*. This Filipino tradition of travelers bringing gifts from their destination to people back home for family or friends, an endearing tradition practiced for centuries helps strengthen family ties and friendships. She feels she can't get away from this, especially since she has been away for several years. The whole block in her city has to be allotted something special. Oh, my … she has to shop at Costco to save on items that she can bring back home. A few aunts want her to just bring them a bag or lipstick, but some are a bit demanding and critical and would make side comments like, *Is that all I get?, I guess I am not that close to you since mine is a cheap gift, or how could you forget me?* So, Beth is making a list even bigger than the ones she makes at Christmas so as not to miss anyone. She plans to gather her high school friends for a small reunion at a beach resort, where she can just give the women make-up kits and the men will be happy if the party is overflowing with San Miguel beer. Of course, a big, roasted pig has to be part of the festivities, or maybe rotisserie chicken as a healthier alternative, along with some freshly caught and broiled fish. She envisions getting the royal treatment from all of them since *balikbayans* who are generous are generally reciprocated with a red carpet welcome. She is also bracing herself, since there will always be someone critical and she can't please everyone.

Financial Literacy, or Lack of It

My client Rose has a brother who she thought was financially stable, since he is an international pilot. Recently, he told Rose's parents that the skies are not as friendly anymore and he wants to be close to his family before his children embark on their college education. He has a five-year business plan to start a barbecue stand that he has sent to Rose and their parents. His friend, he notes, franchised his chicken barbecue business, and is making a lot of money. He thinks his plan is well-thought-out. He has a secret dry rub formula from another pilot friend who hails from Memphis, Tennessee, and the taste is *umm finger-licking good!* He wants to take a loan out against the half million pesos (approximately $10,000) he has saved in the bank, and is pleading with Rose and his parents to help fund his family's monthly expenses while he is building his business.

Rose is very skeptical and has warned her brother not to use his savings for his children's college fund, but it seems like he is firm in his decision. Her husband Rick suggested that Rose give her brother a copy of Suze Orman's *Action Plan Book* to subtly remind him about his responsibility for his own family's financial planning. As Suze writes, "New times calls for new rules," and the book includes chapters on kids, money, and much more. He doesn't want to meddle in Rose's family and money affairs, but he also deeply empathizes with his wife's predicament and is particularly concerned about her parents' and Rose's inability to say no to the family's money demands. A year ago, when Rose's brother visited them in Miami, the brother jokingly told Rose that it would be easy for her to help with his children's college education. "After all, it's not as expensive as here in America, just a couple of hundred dollars per semester," he said. Now Rose's husband is dreading that he will be dragged into this abyss, as well.

Rose is determined to be strict with her budget, but now she feels overwhelmed. Her blood pressure is climbing, and she is dreading talking to her brother. Will she have the *chutzpah* (determination or guts) to say NO if her pilot brother makes his dream business proposal?

How can Beth help her family lower their expectations of financial help from her after several years of giving them money? What else can she do?

Is Rose's kindness partly the reason for her family's financial co-dependency? Where did she go wrong? Will her family ever understand that money doesn't grow on trees in America?

Will Liz's family still love her if she doesn't satisfy all their wants?

All my clients are wondering: "What price will we Filipino nurses (and OFWs) pay to keep the love of our family? Is it worth withdrawing some of our coveted IRA funds or retirement savings to pay for a grand reunion just to maintain peace and harmony and please our families in the Philippines?"

This book will guide you to a path of financial independence and teach you how to avoid the family-money drama by practicing the tools and strategies outlined in the chapters to come. You will no longer have to feel like Beth, both dreading and anticipating a grand reunion vacation and wondering, "Is it really more fun in the Philippines?"

Chapter 3

THE WALKING WOUNDED

"Belle, we have no choice, we have to do an emergency cardiac catheterization on you. There are changes on your EKG, and as you know, with your family history combined with your symptoms of chest pain early this morning and a blood pressure of 200/115, we have to do this *now*."

As a former critical care nurse and ARNP, I understood the interventional cardiologist's sense of urgency; he didn't have to elaborate his findings to me. I gave my beloved husband a big kiss: I was optimistic that with G-d's help, I would emerge from this ordeal. I reminded my husband to call our rabbi for extra prayers, and requested that my nephew, who is an emergency room nurse, keep my husband company while I went through this urgent medical procedure.

The day before my cardiac episode, I had a very stressful day at work. My ardent efforts to be both efficient and empathic with the wife of a client who was battling pancreatic cancer were not enough for her. None of the strategies that I proposed seemed to ensure smooth scheduling of all the required procedures in a way that would satisfy his wife. I kept my emotions to myself with the understanding that as the caretaker, she had gone through so much herself watching her 45-year-old husband suffer. As the nurse coordinator, I had to be ultra-empathic.

I had already contemplated resigning because this dream career that I had envisioned was not how it was in actuality. My supervisor had requested that I rethink my decision, and had dangled an even more lucrative position to tempt me to stay. Of course, I felt guilty. I reconsidered, but I was emotionally and physically exhausted, and my drive and stamina were diminishing. Still I worried that my departure from my old familiar life as a nurse would be devastating financially, emotionally, and mentally. How would my family in Miami get by? How would my extended family in the Philippines manage without my constant financial help?

Then I landed in the emergency room and in surgery. After my recuperation, my attempts to resume my nursing career were met with sky-rocketing blood pressure every time I attempted to go back to work. I took yoga classes, had monthly massages, and practiced aerobic exercises three or four times a week at the gym. Living a healthy lifestyle, just like the mantra I teach my patients. Nothing helped, and physicians were bewildered. They modified my anti-hypertensive medications, but the hypertension persisted; deep inside I was aware that my physical body did not agree with my rational mind. My heart whispered something else to me. It was a very quiet sound, yet profound and clear. "I need to do something else, I want to make a difference in this world, I'm born to do something more joyful and meaningful." My belief was and is that "*to actualize your G-d-given gifts is a prerequisite to attain a meaningful and joyful life.*" What that would be, I didn't then know.

Family and colleagues couldn't understand why I wanted to change careers or scale back after I left my university job. Many were condescending, telling me that I was wasting my graduate school degree. I can understand their disappointment. Recruiters were everywhere, and with a resume as diverse as mine, I could have landed a six-figure salary. But I wanted to be my authentic self.

I embarked on a mission to understand what my true calling was. First, I took a solo trip back to the Philippines to reconnect with my roots. After super-typhoon Haiyan or Yolanda, which hit my province of Leyte, my husband and I had partnered with an Israel-based NGO (non-government organization) to empower farmers in the restoration of agricultural lands in memory of my father, who was the former regional director for the Bureau of Soils. My dream, since my youth, was to uplift the economic situation of the poor and destitute. As a child, I loved talking to our farmer-tenants, and I dreamed of strategies for how to bridge the gap, be they education as my mother envisioned, or business know-how and mentorship like *Shark Tank*. Since I'd always wanted to serve my community, I thought of dragging my husband along as well, but I knew he wasn't ready—truthfully, neither was I. The project we collaborated on is thriving and has increased the farmers' income at least seven-fold. For those who are curious, here's the link: www. globalgiving.org/17225.

It took years of self -assessment, soul-searching, deep self-introspection, and, thankfully, a guiding light to allow me to forge my own destiny. I took very transformative weekly classes on spirituality and connected with the true calling that spoke to me from the core of my being. There were many "aha" moments and various change catalysts. It wasn't easy, but I persisted and the results are metamorphic. My soul is now able to express itself clearly and is very happy. Now, I want this message to resonate to other Filipino nurses who are struggling silently. *You are not alone.*

I invested in myself, and went on a mission that focused on personal and spiritual growth and empowerment. I can't count the number of books I've read that have influenced my thought processes and way of dealing with setbacks and challenges in life.

I take Torah classes weekly, but that is my choice and my path. I'm just informing you that I indulge in learning more deeply to tap into my soul. I respect anyone's choice of how to tap into your core being. The fact that you are reading this right now says you are meant to hear my message, and especially the tools and strategies that I will provide you. I know you are hurting, and of course, that is the reason I wrote this book: to empower you and get you out of the conundrum where you are right now. Suffer no more, I will be with you in your journey!

Watching other women, especially the *rebbetzins* (rabbis' wives) who seemed to have purposeful and joyful lives was not enough for me. I wanted the same thing to happen to myself! So,

I learned one on one from many mentors. Then I encountered a life coach who espoused a lot of the universal laws of morality that I had learned and I was impressed; it was as if she was speaking to the many dilemmas I had with my family-money drama as well. Her words also changed the trajectory of my life profoundly. I had never heard of a life coach before, though I'd read somewhere about coaching or counseling. But, I said, why not? If she was confident she could serve my needs and she was espousing the universal laws of morality, then I was in.

I signed up and paid one-on-one coaching, as well, and the combination of all of the above transformed me holistically. Of course, my husband's unconditional love was always at my side. I am so glad I took care of myself and invested in improving my overall mental, physical, and spiritual health and well-being. It had a profound effect on me and have even transformed my relationships with my family and many others. My spirituality is actually more and more meaningful now and I am truly living a more joyful life.

Around this time is when and how I found the motivation that I felt was the passion and calling I was waiting for. It took me years to extricate myself from the family-money abyss I was in. I know many Filipinos like you in a similar predicament. *I am determined to assist in ways I can to reach as many people who are willing to hear my voice.*

There are many familiar stories that happen daily among Filipino nurses and workers. I don't want you to be alone in dealing with these situations. There are times in your life when we are simply not very good at balancing everything in life as an adult. Even skilled basketball players like Steph Curry, Kevin

Durant, or the king of the hoops, Lebron James, need coaches to orchestrate the game of basketball. This year, Mr. Durant joined the Warriors and got the coveted NBA championship. Lebron James' determination with his team and coach in 2016 delivered the Cleveland Cavalier's first championship ring. It's a game I know most of us Filipinos are familiar with, so whatever team you rooted for, I just want to emphasize that a *coach* was there to guide their offense or defense.

A *life coach* can give you feedback regarding when, how, and where your next moves should be: what to look for, what to avoid, and how to undo old patterns by showing you strategies unique to you. I remember it took a while for my tennis coach to undo my faulty pattern of hitting the tennis balls. If I didn't see him for a month, my tendency was to go back to the old ways, but after a few sessions with him, I was able to get back to the right moves. Then he thought that with the right intensive training I could play with the newly crowned tennis great Serena Williams. Really? Well, maybe after several years more of practice, I can serve her. I didn't say I can beat her of course, not in this lifetime, but I can dream about just playing a game with her. You too can achieve your dreams, be it a joyful life, abundance, peace in the family, or whatever you aspire to if you *are willing to look and change from within to transform your world and truly actualize your own potential.* You can start NOW!

Chapter 4

THE GOALS OF MONEY

> *"You can only become truly accomplished at something*
> *you love. Don't make money your goal. Instead, pursue*
> *the things you love doing, and then do them so well that*
> *people can't take their eyes off you."*
> **MAYA ANGELOU**

Many immigrants, myself included, have dreams of making it big in America. Isn't that the reason why most of us left our native country, our family, and our loved ones? The extra shift differential for night shifts and overtime work are performed by most Filipino nurses in many hospitals due to the monetary reward and despite the many challenges. Let's not fool ourselves: we Filipino nurses and OFWs crave the good things in life, the trimmings that society has *dictated* to us that we *should* possess. We downloaded so many rules from our childhood and have embedded them so deeply inside our minds that the so-called "success the Pinoy way" is to have a big house for our parents in the Philippines, an elegant abode to entertain our friends and colleagues in America, a sleek Mercedes Benz or BMW, experience exotic trips, children who are going to the best private schools—oh, and we also want them to be the smartest and best in class.

How do I know? Of course, I've been there and done my own accumulating, especially during the roaring eighties. My *nouveau riche* mentality took me shopping for Gucci boots and Ferragamo shoes in Rome; experiencing some amazing vistas at Cinque Terre in Italy; and marching the shiny, limestone-paved streets of the city of Dubrovnik, Croatia during a Mediterranean cruise. Though we have no children, I took pride about my smart nephews and nieces who, like many Filipino-American children in my circle, are super-achievers.

We have difficulty breaking free from the shackles of our way of thinking—or we never question them because we grew up watching others do the same. They seemed happy, or at least that was the idea ingrained in us. We have cultural beliefs and practices that dictate to us how to exist as well as how to define success and even happiness. We follow the paths of many people who are called *successful,* but we never pause to think if the meaning of their success applies to our own lives. We generally follow the herd mentality. Some of us were told to obtain a master's degree to get promoted, or an MBA to succeed in the corporate world. Whatever it is, unbeknownst to us, we are influenced by these beliefs, and the media has saturated us as well with all the goods that we "should" have in our lives.

The belief patterns that we were surrounded with, coupled with expectations from the outside world, are difficult to shrug off, but there will come a time when we get exhausted, get stressed out, or just frankly cannot sustain the patterns of living that we thought we had perfectly envisioned for ourselves and our family. Stuff happens, or should I say *sh*t* happens, but don't panic. These things happen to most of us. A few are able to transcend the culture they grew up with, but many continue to do the same thing they're doing. Just like most of my clients who've said, "It's ok, I'm happy," while their tone of voice revealed the exact opposite.

It took them years to hear the internal voice whispering to them to make the changes necessary to take the path less travelled and to fully commit to become empowered with the assistance of a *life coach*. They were miserable with their situation of constantly helping their family even when they could no longer afford to continue sending them monthly assistance. For a while, they ignored the inner voice inside because, in their words, "We don't want a World War III in our family," along with many other reasons. We are creatures of habit, and it is much easier to work extra overtime, or hope and pray that the people we are supporting will change, or wait years until they graduate nursing school or land lucrative jobs, because we think. "They can't do it on their own yet, maybe when …."

We have to conquer our fears. We want the security of our nursing careers, or the comfort of not dealing with our family and just keeping the status quo. Although we have reservoirs of resilience that can be tapped, our families have their own reservoir as well, so let us not keep them buried in the primitive brain, in our amygdala. Incidentally, the amygdala is responsible for the response and memory of emotions, especially fear. Fear controls the way we react to certain stimuli or events that cause emotion: our fear of being ostracized, fear of losing our family connections if we stop helping them, fear of losing the love and respect from our family, and many more. We have to deal with these fears with utmost compassion and understanding of ourselves and the people surrounding us.

Most of us are cognizant that money can't buy love, whether from our family, friends, or parents. Yet most of us subconsciously are doing just that. We buy gifts for graduations, birthdays, weddings. We buy souvenirs or *pasalubong*. Sometimes, we may even buy gifts that we can't afford just to please the recipient. We *think* that the recipients of our gifts or financial assistance will respect or love us unconditionally, but the truth is that some do truly love us and respect us, but many do not. You will see this for yourself the moment you set limits or turn off the money spigot. Then you will know who your family or friends really are.

Without consciously thinking about it, many of us are not aware that we may have been living our life to *please so many people* here and back in our home country. Some of them are appreciative of what you've done for them, others, as I've said, are not. Some calculated that with your current income, you could have given them more, maybe buy them a car or at least cover the down payment for one, not to mention other *stuff* that they would like to possess. Many have estimated that, based on your current income, you could easily fund the education of all your nephews and nieces. My clients Liz, Rose, and Eva were expected to do just this.

Initially, the financial assistance requests boosted your ego, and you want to help, of course. We espouse "Love your brother as thyself," we need to share our bounty and help those who need assistance. But then slowly, like many OFWs, you feel the pressure and start getting annoyed that some family members are in a path of co-dependency. Liz's niece, who she had sent to college and who then landed a job in Qatar, called and demanded that Liz pay her airfare when she had difficulty adjusting to her job in the Middle East. She wanted to come back to the Philippines, and threatened to blame Liz if something happened to her when Liz refused to pay for her airfare back home. What *chutzpah*! (That's Liz's actual word!) Needless to say, Liz cut off communications with her sister's family for a few years because of these shenanigans. Once you set boundaries, tensions start to rise, the phone calls or FB messages are not as friendly anymore. Then resentments, anger, and emotional hurt ensue. A typical scenario that occurs among Filipino nurses includes a subtle rise of blood pressure and other stress-related ailments, and then family dynamics start morphing into obvious signs of emotional pain and suffering that affects the whole family and even the younger generation.

"Too many people spend money they earned … to buy things they don't want to impress people that they don't like."
WILL ROGERS

When you start getting serious about acknowledging what your goal really is for your money, you may encounter many challenges within yourself and in your environment, and I can assure you some of them are not going to be *pretty!* But if you can change your perspective, tweak some rules, and even ignore most of them, you will encounter many "aha" moments, and you will be surprised that you can soar to heights you have never thought you can achieve in your life. You will experience joy and *abundance in life.*

One of the prerequisites of changing your perspective is to truly FORGIVE. This word has seven letters, and in *Kabbalah* (the soul of the Torah, an ancient Jewish tradition that teaches the deepest insights into the essence of G-d, His interaction with the world, and the purpose of Creation), the number seven has much significance, an example of which is the seven days of creation.5 This acronym, **FORGIVE,** and its accompanying steps to help you, will be detailed in the succeeding chapters:

F—Focus on Self-Awareness and Self-Love. In an airplane, we are instructed to put our mask first before we assist our children or other loved ones, hence we need to start from within ourselves.

O—Obliterate Emotional Cords. Unbeknownst to many of us, we have *cords of attachments* to people in our lives. We contribute negative patterns into that cord and the other person does too. The energies of the cord affect us subconsciously in a variety of ways. They send negative patterns back and forth between you, leaving you feeling haunted by these traumatic experiences. *When you set boundaries and cut a cord of attachment, you are removing or lifting the negative behavioral,* *emotional, and mental patterns that circulate between you and the other person.* We have emotions about our family, loved ones, friends, acquaintances, co-workers, and people we encounter daily that affect how we manifest abundance as well as how we share our bounty.

R—Remove Money Blocks. Oftentimes, the reason we can't achieve our own abundance in money or love is because we have blocks that have hindered us from manifesting what we desire in our life. Many are subtle, and because we have practiced them for so long in our lives, we don't think they are blocks to manifesting abundance. You'll be surprised to know that these can easily be removed by reading Chapter 6.

G—Gratitude and Give Back. The importance and significance of gratitude and giving back is well-documented, but I do have a few additions to the arsenal on this topic and will guide you how to make a powerful, daily gratitude journal.

I—In G-d We Trust. (Spirit, Divine Creator, the Universe, Eternal Light etc.). *"You open your hand and satisfy the desire of every living thing. The Lord is righteous in all His ways, and benevolent in all His deeds. The Lord is close to all who call upon Him, to all who call upon Him in truth."*—Psalm 145:16-18

V—Value Yourself. Self-respect is one of the most crucial aspects we need to master in life. If you don't know how to truly value yourself and appreciate your self-worth, how do you expect others to respect and value you?

E—Envision Your Future and Enhance Your System of Living. Change is not easy, but in this chapter, I will provide you with ways to upgrade your current system of living. Once you master the art of living joyfully, mindfully, and attracting money flow and achieving abundance, sharing your bounty or helping someone in the family may not be an issue for you any longer. Of course, it goes without saying, that you need to be cognizant of co-dependency in the family, and we will address that, too.

"The weak can never forgive.
Forgiveness is the attribute of the strong."
MAHATMA GANDHI

Chapter 5

FOCUS ON SELF-AWARENESS AND SELF-LOVE

"People first, then money, then things. Give to yourself as much as you give of yourself. This means you have to put yourself first. A big part of financial freedom is having your heart and mind free from worry about the what-ifs of life."
SUZE ORMAN

The internationally known personal finance guru is famously quoted for the above statements, and it is probably one of the reasons why she is richer than most of us. Her quotes resonate with so many people, and finance magazines such as *The Motley Fool* have mentioned her many times on money, family, love, and happiness. She is known to not splurge on items that she could have easily afforded; she doesn't buy stuff just to show off. I remember reading in *The Wall Street Journal* about the purchase of her condominium in New York; she could have easily afforded the one with the better view, but she opted for the more affordable one in the same building. Her books were some of the first finance books I perused when I came to this country, and I'm hoping your household has one or two. If not, try to watch her shows on public television. You will get lots of money tips and tools that will empower you to take care of yourself first. (Note: I don't get any royalties from her book sales.) After we take care of our own finances first, then we can take care of others in our family, our community, and the world.

Years ago, a nurse colleague thought it funny when his sister immigrated from the Philippines with her teenage daughters, who brought their iPhones and iPads, when at the time, my colleague was actively saving to purchase just one. His sister, who he was helping financially every month, apparently had money for these gadgets, and my colleague couldn't afford one. If this scenario is too familiar to you, then I may have unnerved you, but I hope you can comprehend this reverse scenario. Oftentimes, we Filipino workers or OFWs withhold our own necessities or luxuries for the sake of our relatives. I used to postpone my haircuts and pedicures so I could send money back home. Was I that crazy? We do need to make a clear delineation between what is luxury and what is necessity. Personally, I had made boundaries about this situation in the past. In the early eighties, a distant relative asked me to give her a Nikon camera as her *pasalubong* on my first trip back home. At that time, it was around $800, and I just flatly said, "I don't even have one because I can't afford it."

We have to learn to say no, and get clear that a no means NO, period. People back in the country also need to understand our predicament here in the USA. As the old cliché goes, "until they walk in your shoes," they will not understand what immigrants do to penny pinch and save money to help the family.

There are so many stories of Filipino nurses and OFWs sending financial assistance to the Philippines while they suffer in poverty in the foreign country where they are working. When relatives or friends demand that we need to help, or that we have to bring them souvenirs and throw big parties when we come home, we should take charge of the situation and learn to curtail it. I know it isn't easy, especially if other people start gossiping about us not being generous, but we need to ignore the noise. In fact, I know I will have many critics for writing this book. I made myself vulnerable so we can open this dialogue. We have to respect our culture, but at the same time, we can modify our extravagance. This requires our own *deep introspection about money.* The change must start from within each of us. We can show our *kababayans* (fellow Filipinos) that we can live within our means.

"You must be the change you want to see in the world."
MAHATMA GANDHI

Easier said than done, right? As they say, if you have the will, you will have the way. But there are myriad factors to consider of why we can't, don't, or postpone the process of changing. I know, because it took me years to do it. Most of us will wait for a defining moment or a catastrophic event before we wake up to the reality, but by then, it may be too late. Don't be like many of us who waited for that moment. Old habits are comfortable. It is difficult for us to let go, or we distract ourselves with busyness, focusing on pleasing others. Our *inner self* may have felt the discomfort of sending money we can't afford, but our ego's fear of being ostracized is so overpowering that we think it's best not to face our demons, and we stay in the status quo. We make up so many excuses. Many women have reached out to me with their family-money issues. Regrettably, some of them aren't ready to make the leap to cross that bridge.

If we have fat bank accounts, monthly royalties or dividends, or other sources of income, perhaps we don't mind working extra hours—to each his or her own. We have free will. We can love ourselves by taking care of our finances first; we do have a choice. Most of us have limited our ability to earn money, and we don't expand our minds to the hundreds of ways to reach our American dream.

When I left my stressful job and relied on my husband's income, we quickly changed our lifestyle. We sold our older, rarely driven second car and shared just one. It was an adjustment, especially when one of us had to run an errand. However, we adjusted over time, and actually loved taking the Miami-Dade County Metro-rail system or the bus. Some so-called friends and acquaintances made fun of us, but we didn't let their comments influence us. We listened to our cheerleaders and spent less time socializing with those who were not fans of our lifestyle.

When I went back to work part-time, we adjusted our schedule. My husband would wake up a bit earlier, drop me off at work, and then continue on to work himself. I took the bus or Uber back home. Luckily, I also had a good friend and colleague, Jian Moses (thanks, Jimo), who dropped me off at the Metro-rail system most of the time. We worked it out.

We stopped going out to the movies every week and switched to Netflix, having movies mailed to us. We found out that much of the entertainment we enjoyed could be had for free, or for a nominal fee. The New World Symphony in Miami Beach has some programs on Sundays that are free to the public, and to reciprocate, we give donations we can afford. The Perez Art Museum has one free Thursday a month, so I entertained most of our out-of-town guests by visiting this Herzog and de Meuron architectural gem in Miami; they were all so pleased with this insider tourist attraction. We deleted our old patterns of spending, since we were realistic about our income. Many people who called themselves our friends stopped calling us, but we did not get bogged down by what others thought.

When many of us run into financial trouble here in America, we dig into our savings, work double shifts, go to the bank, take out a loan, or maybe borrow from credit cards, which we then have to pay back with interest. Of course, no one will believe that you have financial problems, so think about having a clear and conscious conversation, and then leaving it be if you can't convince them.

Likewise, if family members have similar situations back home, they, too, can learn to adjust their income, go to the bank, or work extra to pay for it if they have no savings. But what do most Filipino relatives do? They call us for more money and treat nurses and OFWs as their bank account. Of course, we want to help. But, have you ever asked if they have tried to save even 10% of what you have been sending them? Oh, they can't or don't want to save, right? Do they have bank accounts so they'll learn how to save, establish their credit, and can take loans? In fact, the act of taking out life insurance for their children or spouses can jumpstart their financial literacy. Better yet, gift them one of Suze Orman's books, one of the least expensive yet most important tools we can provide to help open their eyes about financial responsibilities. The only way to change is to show by example and be mindful. Let go of patterns of behavior that we are used to doing to please our family and social circle.

On the other hand, there are brain hacks we can leverage to change our outlook about money. How many of us have been told that *"money doesn't grow on trees,"* or that *"money is the root of all evil"*? These subconscious beliefs will be discussed in later chapters so that you can start reprogramming your mind. We have to be filled first before we can share, and if we share, it has to come from the heart. We only want to give willingly and joyfully, not expecting anything in return and not using the giving process to control others. The universe is generous. We'll delve further into that later.

I know, I know, I can hear you telling me, "Belle, we have to tiptoe when we stop helping family members financially so we don't damage our relationships." To recap, there are many ways to help families, such as giving cash gifts only for holidays or special occasions, helping them set up a realistic budget based on their income and expenses, prepaying their bills or a car payment if they are behind, feeding them or providing them with jobs until they can find one suitable for their qualifications.

We assisted family members and provided a job to an in-law when they had just arrived here in America. You can help your family members by walking them through employment application forms that they may not be familiar with, or hiring them to take care of your lawn or garden, if you can afford to pay them. Most of the time, they will also take pride that they are doing something in return—not all the time, of course, especially if they are not used to doing chores back home.

You can also help by modifying this for your relatives back home in the Philippines. I'm cognizant of the possible resistance, which I have heard often enough. From the many stories related to me, I know that many relatives may be reluctant to do the work or feel that it is beneath them to do menial tasks, so I'm aware that this has to be approached delicately and with true compassion and understanding of our *Pinoy* pride.

Have you noticed that no one confronts the family member or members who chronically get behind financially in the first place? Instead, the person who constantly gives (the giver) is designated unofficially and *repeatedly* to provide monetary assistance to the same person or family members (they would be the takers) who need financial aid. As you are reading this, analyze your own family dynamics and list the givers and the takers in your family. We want to feel compassion for those who need our assistance during health crises or emergencies, but when we observe that a taker is not a good steward of his/ her money, then we have to rethink the process of altruism in the family. We are all familiar with the idea that "charity begins at home," but many times, we have to battle guilt and shame.

I know this is a subject that is a taboo in Filipino conversations. Hence, I have shared a few tools to empower you when this situation occurs. The strategies outlined below will help anyone successfully find their path with the least resistance and avoid the much-dreaded prolonged family feud.

There are many ways to *love and take care* of ourselves. As nurses, we have been inundated with ads for deep tissue massages, the importance of exercise, and the benefits of yoga and meditation. Focusing on healthy, green vegetables and low-carb diet, listening to music, going to plays, jogging in the park, or talking to a life coach are some of the ways to ventilate, relax, and contemplate, especially if a family member has bullied you for not giving them money immediately. For some people, clothes shopping, swimming, biking, crocheting, or engaging in hobbies help get them out of the doldrums. Spend more time at your organic garden, or just do a daily brisk walk to clear your mind. Avoid guilt, anger, and feeling resentful.

Talking of anger and resentment, *forgiveness* is crucial to be able to release these emotions and start taking care of oneself. Deleting this negative energy is a *must* so you can move on. Some people can shrug off situations nonchalantly or by doing the activities mentioned above, but for many of us, anger may stay in our systems for a long time if we perceive that our kindness was manipulated or taken for granted. Often this requires deep soul- searching; otherwise, these feelings will stay in our system and, unbeknownst to us, they will obstruct the flow of money to our coffers. There's plenty of money around, but self- introspection and reflection is a must before one creates prosperity. As nurses, we can assess our own physical and emotional symptoms. Evaluate your irritable emotions, body malaise, exhaustion, poor appetite or over-eating, sleepless nights, feelings of depression, or hypertension. All of them can be related to one's inability to truly forgive.

As an exercise on awareness, get a sheet of paper and write down the names of the givers and takers in your family, the different reasons for the takers needing financial rescue, and how many times a year the givers and takers in your family interact about money. Are you the giver or are you the taker? If you are the giver, do you take care of your needs first before sending money to the relatives back home, or are you deep in credit card debt but because the relative or family member (*taker*) texted you that they need money, you softened your heart and took the bait?

If you did not give money, how was the interaction with the taker? Did it cause a rift? Is there still love and warmth in your communications with them even after you set limits, or are they ignoring your Facebook posts or not calling you back any longer? Do you continue to get holiday cards and birthday greetings?

We have to take care of our emotions that come up over this financial strife. Let's go over the list and start looking at their names. Imagine that you are truly forgiving them. First, connect to G-d or eternal light or Holy Spirit (or whatever your belief is on spirituality, no judgment here). Then, think about each person and say his or her name out loud: "I forgive you, _____." Ask them to forgive you, too, and send these people blessings for a great day. Take note of how you feel about them and of any gradual changes you observe. As you practice this exercise, jot down the progress you notice within yourself.

"Neither a borrower nor a lender be. For loan oft loses both itself and friend, and borrowing dulls the edge of husbandry."
POLONIUS, *HAMLET* BY WILLIAM SHAKESPEARE, **1602**

Chapter 6

OBLITERATE EMOTIONAL CORDS

Before we take on this emotionally charged chapter, let's review some of the reasons why we send money to our family back in the country:

- Educate a family member (brother, sister, nephew, niece, cousin)—this is one of the most compelling reasons
- Fund our parents' retirement
- Provide capital for the business of a family member
- Establish a medical emergency fund for loved ones who are ill
- Provide monthly financial assistance to family members with limited sources of income
- Pay for the medications of family members

I'm sure there are many other logical reasons why we all send money to our family. Some of us may have been helping since we arrived in America, perhaps as long as five or more years ago. We follow no rules about how long we should help them or what is the appropriate amount.

In my early days, I just sent as much as I can afford— sometimes more than 25% of my net income. At the time, I truly did not mind, since my goal was to educate as many people as I could in the belief that education would get them out of poverty and no one would be left behind. Collectively, in our immediate family, we've educated a few nurses, engineers, a veterinary doctor, a geologist, and other professionals. However, times are changing when it comes to education. The advent of many online educational tools, some of which are free or easily accessible, and other practical means of enhancing income should be part of our arsenal. Just as we do in taking care of patients, we have to incorporate a holistic approach when assisting our families. Most of us are stuck in our old ways. By not getting out of our comfort zones, we are creating financial co-dependency in many family members. Then, as the years pass and sustainability of financial largess is of necessity abruptly stopped, family relationships crumble, creating craters of deep emotional wounds. Most of us have been there. From talking to many colleagues, acquaintances, and clients, I hear that the wounds are getting deeper and deeper. Contrary to the old adage that "time heals all wounds," emotional shrapnel will follow us wherever we go until it is cared for and addressed properly.

Occasionally, there may be some family bullies who will pressure us to constantly dole out money and are inconsiderate of the changes in our own financial situation. Let's face it, these bullies have their own agenda, which could be to satisfy their own ego. Or perhaps they just want to show off that they are very successful and that they can share their bounty. Often, they may appear as the matriarch or patriarch in charge of and mindful of everyone's budget—except yours. Sometimes they forget where they come from or who gave them the crutches when they were once down and crippled. I know this is too familiar for many of you. But watch these family bullies: Do they really give to those who are in need? This will require your full attention when bullies show up. If you are truly maxed out and cannot give, then you just have to be honest. Complaining will not get us anywhere, it stops the *energy flow* and may send us into reversal. Our families have expectations based on their knowledge of how much a nurse or any professional makes, which is just one Google search away on the Internet. Let's not waste our energy trying to reason this out with our demanding family member; be bold enough to say, "I am not able to help at this time," and then try to move on. Was that really hard to say? I know … it is…

Emotional wounds literally hurt; the word *heartache* is not just a metaphor. Most of us drag those wounds around like a sack of rice pulling us from behind and slowing us down, preventing us from moving forward in our lives. Many women have told me that everything is now OK between them and whichever family member they had a spat with, but when I probe deeper, it turns out they haven't talked to each other for three or more years because of family-money drama. I knew someone who had not talked to her mother for more than 15 years until the mother was on her deathbed! We Filipinos love to show off how great our lives are, but we have mastered the art of using a Band-Aid on the emotional wounds we carry around. No matter how big the bandage, as far as our neurons are concerned, emotional distress is still ongoing physical trauma.

First off, we have to revisit our old self. We may even have to go deep in our psyche to when we were less than 10 years old. Sometimes, things that happened in our childhood are needles that constantly prick at our brains and cause pain. Deep cleansing may be just what the doctor ordered.

I remember a patient of mine who had undergone two kidney transplants, and when she was about to be discharged, she got febrile and later went into septic shock. After thorough probing and many cultures, the culprit was discovered to be a tiny internal wound that had become infected and was only detected after a CT scan. Of course, the experienced surgeon had to reopen the incision to get to the bottom of the infected wound and personally cleaned this wound twice a day! I was in awe of the surgeon's dedication. Like this world-renowned transplant surgeon, we have to really put in the effort, energy, time, and money to clean our emotional wounds.

After we search for those emotional wounds lurking within us, we have to find an empathic, compassionate, and understanding person who is willing to hear our story and truly listen with her/his heart. Acknowledgment is actually one of the steps to care and love yourself[6]. A recounting of your experiences, including the emotional reactions you had, should be included in this dialogue. Don't hold back from any emotional pain or suffering you went through; this is your time to vent and express yourself fully. Make sure this is a person you feel good opening up to, someone you feel comfortable having a meaningful conversation with. In most situations, a professional person who is experienced to handle your situation is best, but if you find comfort in a trusted or sympathetic friend, then that can also help. Remember my patient, however. *I strongly suggest you hire the best-trained surgeon to treat this infection and be willing to pay his/her professional charges.*

The all-too-familiar stages of the grieving process—denial, anger, grief, and acceptance—are a common experience when healing emotional trauma, but contrary to what we learned as nurses, the path to acceptance takes quite some time to reach. Most are stuck in the denial stage for a long time. Sometimes they never get over it and will just live out their lives unhappy, unfulfilled, and less abundant. Some spend so much of their waking hours grieving that they can no longer appreciate anything good in their lives; the grief has overpowered their whole way of living. Sometimes in the stages of denial, anger or grief reoccur before acceptance is reached. I've witnessed this, too, and often my clients will believe outside factors are the cause of their melancholy or distress. They'll tell me that having a nasty boss, working in a difficult environment, being married to a lazy spouse, parenting unruly children, or factors beyond their control are making them miserable. It is so difficult for them to see that their power is *right there,* within their core being, to help them see the light. They deny themselves the path to happiness and manifesting abundance in their lives, which are actually all within their reach.

There are a number of obstacles that we must become aware of and remain present to in our daily living and in our relationships. One of these obstacles is our *ego,* which wants to control our lives. Our ego is addicted to being in power and in control of our present moment, and it has its tricks to seduce our minds. Our ego makes it difficult to dismiss the voice in our head or self-talk. The thoughts feel like they are your thoughts so many of us feel like we are stuck with our personalities such as being '*hot tempered*' or '*shy*' or '*sad*' and that these are fixed traits. Another ego trick is that our ego believes it is not safe from *life*, that life is dangerous. It therefore insists on controlling the events of life; surrender is perceived as an enemy of the ego, something dangerous. Fear is the ego's most powerful weapon since it can distort truth and peace, create confusion or fracture and separate people. So watch out for these ego tricks. Many have fallen deep into the abyss because of too much ego, so we have to learn when to admit when we are wrong and look within ourselves to see how we can heal our own wounded feelings before we can expect others to fix theirs. Oftentimes, our speech patterns, our words, or how we reacted are culprits in miscommunication or broken feelings within our families. Love is the only true way out but our ego tries to convince us that love is weakness.

One of the roads less travelled to obliterating emotional cords in our lives is awareness that everything happens by *Divine Providence,* and hence will benefit us later. So when something happens that is painful in life, instead of getting very emotional and angry, we can ask ourselves: *Why did this situation happen to me? Did this happen to refine me? Is this an opportunity for me to accomplish something unexpected?* The biblical figure who personifies this attitude in an outstanding way is Joseph. His brothers had sold him into slavery and he languished in an Egyptian jail, but he eventually became the viceroy of Egypt, and when his brothers finally came to Egypt, they were dependent on his mercy and power. After the death of their father, Jacob, the brothers feared that Joseph, whom they so hated and who was now so powerful, would exact revenge. But, as Joseph tells them*: Do not Fear, everything that happened with me was G-d's plan in order to bring salvation to all.*

Cutting emotional cords to people who may have hurt us emotionally may change our perspective toward them. We may need to grieve over the loss of that relationship, and it can be hard to hold onto the memories of fun times we had with them. Setting boundaries with people who hurt us emotionally is reasonable to do.

We tend to have significant emotional cords attached to family members, parents, siblings, our spouse, children: the people who have made significant impact on our emotions. When we cut an emotional cord with a person, it doesn't mean we are cutting off our relationship or familial bonds. It only changes our energy field and emotions. We are no longer willing to be emotionally blackmailed by these family members. We are allowing more good stuff to come into our life. We are releasing the emotional connection and connecting from a clean slate. We are now respecting their journey in life. It doesn't impact on the other person because they have their own *free will.*

This is one of the most effective ways in dealing with emotional pain within families without the usual verbal confrontations that sometimes create even more traumatic exchanges between family members. If you are thinking of cutting a cord of attachment to someone in your family, kindly email me at www.Familyabundancecoach.com so I may be able to discuss this technique with you in more detail, or PM me on Facebook.

$$\boxed{\text{Chapter 7}}$$

REMOVE HIDDEN
MONEY BLOCKS

Gossip

The Philippines' national pastime, OMG! And we take pride in this? No worries, most of us have done this at some time in our lives, myself included, and some of us have done this more often than not. Unfortunately, this is an addiction that we need to detox ourselves from. Gossip is a vicious rumor that violates the sacred space of another person. We make jokes about it as just a little comment about other people that seems innocent, but we don't realize these benign-sounding comments are actually detrimental. We are not discussing this topic as a form of judgment of ethics and values but rather, we want to highlight this common, but serious, flaw that we Filipinos too often make light of.

Most of us fail to realize that good old gossip can be a block to the flow of our financial abundance. Did you know? When did you know? I didn't know until I read many books, engaged in deep self-introspection, and learned from mentors and life coaches. How does gossip block our flow from the eternal source? First, let us discuss gossip briefly and see if you can relate.

- Gossip can harm other people; has anyone hurt you because of gossip?
- Spreading rumors or divulging negative opinions of someone to another person can come from our own place of jealousy, insecurity, pain and low self-esteem.
- Even if you're not a gossiper and just simply want to listen to coworkers so as not to be rude or just to get along, this is still an act of gossip. *Active listening* actually supports and promotes gossiping since if there was no listener, then there would be no audience to promote that gossipy behavior.
- Work gossip is often fueled by ulterior motives and can significantly damage someone's career. Lies can tarnish the reputation of the subject or person.
- If you hear someone gossip about someone else, chances are they gossip about you, too.
- Harm done by speech can never be repaired.
- Human beings have *free will*, it is up to us to discern whether to stop the gossip right there or let it spread. We can nip it in the bud!

Speech is the tool of creation; when G-d blew a soul into Adam, he became a 'speaking being' (Genesis 2:7)[7]. The driving force of humanity is verbal interaction, hence we need to guard our unique attribute of speech. Through speech, we can build up individuals with praise and encouragement. By making others feel important, we validate them as if to say, *your existence is necessary*. This is life-giving and life-affirming. Consider the biblical story of Miriam, Moses' sister, who contracted *tzaraas*, (commonly mistranslated as leprosy, it's actually more a physical manifestation of spiritual deficiency) after she spoke *loshon hara* (gossip) about her brother Moses (Numbers ch.12).

Gossip is a block to our manifestation because it separates us from each other. We are commanded to "love thy brother as thyself," but if we hurt someone through gossip and create distance between people, then our souls are not vessels for the Divine Creator or Source to provide us the blessings for which we ask. We are not ready to receive them. Imagine a dirty container filled with junk: Where can you put a luscious fruit or scrumptious cake? Do you want to put them in the same container, or would you prefer a clean plate where you can savor all the flavors of the fruit and cake and enjoy the experience fully?

So, we have to clean our own vessels first before we can clean others' containers to be worthy of receiving manifestations of an abundant life. The first step in avoiding *Lashon Hara* is to recognize our own faults and commit to improving on them. When we accept responsibility for our inadequacies, then we will be less critical and more tolerant of others. The tongue is an instrument so dangerous it is kept hidden from view behind two protective walls, the mouth and teeth, to prevent its misuse.

Once something escapes your tongue, you can't take it back. Self-refinement benefits the community we live in as well as making us a vehicle in which the divine providence and G-d or Source (or whichever term you use) resides and sends his blessings.

Jealousy and Sibling Rivalry

"Thou shalt not covet thy neighbor's wife, or his male or female servant, his ox or donkey, or anything that belongs to your neighbor." (Exodus chapter 20:17). The prohibition against desiring forbidden things is also seen as a moral imperative for the individual to exercise control over the thoughts of his mind and the desires of his heart. I'll refrain from discussing in detail the Ten Commandments or the Universal Laws of Morality here. My aim is just a gentle reminder and to relate this law to the ingrained Filipino culture of envy that is so difficult to shake off. (I am not a scholar on both of the above either, many books have been written and each of us can choose our paths to enlightenment. References are provided for everyone to review this very important universal law of morality.).

As you know, jealousies and sibling rivalries are still moral minefields in this generation, and from the observations and experiences of many of us, these two demons are still plagues that destroy many of our families. Desire of things that we can't yet afford or possess can lead to coveting. It can even lead to stealing.

Sibling rivalry controls our mind when we pack our overflowing *balikbayan* boxes and try to make sure that our souvenirs for our brothers and sisters back home are of similar quantity or of the same price. We are sensitive to their feelings, and know that one might get jealous of the other. And by the way, no matter what, some recipients will still complain that they deserved a better souvenir or that the other person got the better deal. We just can't make everyone happy! In fact, by not honoring the individuality of our families back home due to our own fears of allowing jealousy to surface within our households, we make ourselves vulnerable to criticisms—and we're not supporting the uniqueness of each person. We don't allow our authentic selves to show up because we are concerned of the possible jealousy we might create within our family.

To be vulnerable means showing strength in what we believe is right. Many times, coveting someone else's sleek new car, Chanel bag, new house, or any possession that overseas Filipino workers saved for years to purchase is the cause of many family feuds. I don't intend to be your morality police, but I hope that we, and I mean us OFWs and especially those left behind in the Philippines, can monitor the *Jealousy* or *Jello meter* that is present in all of us so that we can be our own force for change. Our thoughts and actions count. Let us not let the green-eyed monster dictate what it craves, but let us each have our own moral compass so we can receive the blessings that we all richly deserve. We do not need to compare and contrast with other people, especially with our siblings. *Each of us were born with unique abilities to actualize our lives to our full potential.*

Anger and Resentment

This is another block of which we need to be aware. Let's be honest: If we are sending money regularly over a period of time, we will get resentful, especially if our budget gets tight for whatever reason. We all have been there when an extra $400 could have been used to pay for our mortgage or car payments, but due to family financial obligations, our resources got tapped out. Anger and resentments ensue, and unfortunately, they block our money flow. These could come in layers and may take a while to remove, especially if we have been sitting on them for years. Unless we actively face these demons or get someone to discuss and point this out to us, we may not even be cognizant of their presence.

This has happened to a few clients who thought they had accepted their family-money issues, but the truth was that they gradually harbored feelings of resentment as the years passed—especially when, after assisting with the college education of a nephew or a niece, they were then asked to help another one. They just didn't know when or if it would ever stop, or in which generation it would cease. They shut down their money flow! These money blocks are monsters that hide in many places and can manifest in occasional body aches, in impatience, hypertension, irritability, or other signs of health issues. Once they take root, they are not easy to extract, and there could be layers of them. It can help to have the guidance of a life coach to empower one back to a positive money flow.

Other forms of abundance blocks are belief patterns we learned by osmosis from our parents, grandparents, or other significant members of our family. How many times have you heard from your mother or father that *you have to work hard for your money*, or that *money is the root of all evil*? Different religions have different outlooks about money, and some of these old beliefs may have been downloaded to your subconscious without your full awareness of it. They are preventing you from receiving that flow for prosperity.

Here's a practical game that will help you stop the habit of gossip among friends. Practice this with your close friends with whom you generally talk on a weekly or regular basis, and assign a specific day that you will designate as your NO GOSSIP day. For example, you could decide that each Sunday from 4 to 9 p.m., one of your friends will be assigned to be watchful and very conscious of her speech. The first person in your group could be assigned the first hour, from 4 to 5 p.m., for *one hour of not speaking anything negative about anybody.* If she thinks of saying something negative, she has to think of sending this person blessings. Then the next friend could be assigned to do the same from 6 to 7 p.m., and so on. You can text each other to remind the next person that it is now her turn. Observe how you feel, and discuss any changes among your friends. Do you feel better not talking or judging anyone?

For those who are interested in learning more about how to improve character traits and personalities, you can search Chana Rachel Schusterman's topic on the *Kabbalah of self-refinement,* which is usually studied before the Ten Commandments are given during the Jewish holiday of Shavuot[8] (this coincides with the festival of *Pentecost* in Christian communities).

Chapter 8

GRATITUDE
AND GIVE BACK

*"Gratitude unlocks the fullness of life. It turns what
we have into enough, and more. It turns denial into
acceptance, chaos to order, confusion to clarity. It can
turn a meal into a feast, a house into a home, a stranger
into a friend."*
MELODY BEATTIE

Gratitude

Oh, this is a biggie for me! As I was growing up, my
mother instilled in me the importance of gratitude
and counting my blessings. Sounds familiar, right?
But, guess what? During my years of downward spiral, when

I was annoyed, angry, financially challenged, and resentful, *I was also always complaining about my life!* And, the more I complained, the more things got worse. Our car broke down and we had to cough up $5000 for repairs; my health insurance did not pay my medical bills; the air conditioner had problems in the middle of Florida's August heat; and on and on! What was going on?

I was perplexed and so frustrated. Years before my money flow slowed to almost a halt, we really had a fun-filled life. For several years, my husband and I had great joint income, my career was flourishing, and my husband's business was profitable and professionally rewarding. In fact, we had three properties and were saving 15 to 20 percent of our income, often going out to dinner with friends, watching movies twice a week, and giving to charities. Pretty good for a couple who are DINKS (double income no kids)! We travelled often on business class to Asia using our mileage points. I was doling out money to family members without any questions asked. We were cruising to Alaska and the Mediterranean, making a yearly sojourn to Europe, and living the good life! Gradually, the stress of my career and other bugaboos affected us and turned our life upside down. I chose to resign from my job after becoming emotionally drained, and of course, it didn't help that the great recession in America started to affect everyone's pocketbook!

There were many other outside factors that I thought were the culprit. It was *them*, my work, my family, the people I worked with, patients I took care of, my so-called friends— they were the reasons for my problems. At least, that's what I THOUGHT. Notice that capitalized word "thought"! I lost my focus on the things that mattered most to me and forgot to truly appreciate what I had: a very loving husband, my health, daily meals, and so many other good things. I was the biggest dingbat—someone needed to hit me over the head to wake me up! For those who listened to all my complaints, contact me so I can give you a free signed copy of my book as my belated thanks for listening!

I was in a very dark tunnel for several years! Did I say for years? I mean *many years*… I suffered long and hard before I saw specks of light breaking through the dark clouds of my mind. I would have paid thousands to get me out of that tunnel more quickly; it was damp and so dark where I was. Just a few harsh words that questioned my generosity caused my life to spiral out of control! I became almost a recluse because of so many hurt feelings. Nothing was going right and everything bothered me. I was extremely angry, resentful and asked myself, *how can people do this to me when all my life I have been so kind and generous?*

As the saying goes, sometimes you have to hit bottom before you can go higher: descent for the purpose of ascent. It was not easy. I underwent a lot of deep self- introspection, devoured self-help books, and attended countless spiritual lectures to expand the breadth of my understanding of myself and gain more knowledge about human interactions. I learned from rabbis, *rebbetzins*, mentors, life coaches, and many more. This is one of the main reasons I want to share my experiences and send a ray of hope to many who have been disillusioned in life. What does gratitude have to do with this? A lot!

When life throws us curve balls, our dissatisfaction increases gradually, and if we don't practice gratitude consciously, sad events in our lives overpower our emotions and send us into a downward spiral. Just one sad episode could be the trigger that makes us start focusing on the negative feelings we experienced instead of appreciating the awesome experiences or great things we have going in our life. One negative thought leads to another then another, and negativity just surrounds you.

I know turning this around sounds more easily said than done. This is one of the reasons for spending a whole chapter on *gratitude* and *giving back*. The practice of consciously making a gratitude journal for even the smallest blessings in my life has helped me turn my life into one of joy, happiness, and abundance again. The law of attraction caused a paradigm shift in my reality. By being fully mindful of the positive things I had in my life, I created the energetic changes that I wanted to have happen.

Advocates of the law of attraction believe that by focusing on positive and good thoughts, a person brings positive experiences into their life. By *attracting like energy*, a person can improve their own health, wealth, and personal relationships. Learn to feel, feel good. If a feeling ultimately opens the doors to the treasures of the universe, how bad can it be? If you want it enough, you'll learn to feel it. If you want to change the conditions of your life, you have to change your vibrations, so practice until you can change them in a blink[9]. *Think and feel good and it will be good.*

There are many ways to bring more awareness to our gratitude practice. We all know the good health and well-being that gratitude brings, reducing anxiety, decreasing depression, and improving sleep. The practice of gratitude also allows us to stay in the present. When we are grateful, we let go of our past regrets and future expectations and surrender to the NOW, or present moment. If we keep reminding ourselves of the what-ifs and the what-could-have-beens, we become victims of our past. When we practice real and conscious gratitude, more good things flow and good experiences happen to us. We even attract better-quality friends.

Maslow's hierarchy of needs is a great starting point for what to be grateful for in our lives. From the first and most basic physiologic needs, which are food and clothing, we in America (or those OFWs in other countries) have plenty to be thankful for. We can be grateful for a sunny or a balmy day and the food we eat, whether it's a tuna sandwich, pizza, or green salad. Then we can move on to safety and shelter, being grateful for having a house or place to live. I know most of us practice gratitude, but include your feelings when you do gratitude awareness. If you have a spouse or children, think of the positive qualities they possess, stop focusing on the ones that annoy you. After you practice heartfelt gratitude, observe how your interactions with your spouse or kids change. This simple tip alone improves many relationships! *Write a journal of what you want to thank for no matter how small and do write it daily.*

Give Back

Some people have difficulty with this concept of giving back. When I mentioned this to someone, he pointed to the fact that since many of us Filipinos grew up with not much material abundance, we felt deprived, hence we have difficulty sharing what we have.

Another mentioned that there's always a recession in the Philippines, so we have the *mentality of scarcity*, a feeling that we lack in everything. I beg to differ, since there are many charitable Filipinos who have made significant contributions to different causes. Despite the many religions we Filipinos belong to, we all have been exposed to the biblical passages in some form or another, such as *"A tithe of everything from the land, whether grain from the soil or fruit from the trees, belongs to the Lord. Every tithe of the herd and flock, every tenth animal that passes under the Shepherd's rod, will be holding to the Lord."* Tithing our wealth expresses our awareness that everything we possess really belongs to the Divine Creator and must be used for holy purpose. (Numbers 18; 21-23, Genesis 14:1-20). Some people tithe by saving 10 percent for themselves; others are obligated as part of their religious practices. Again, no judgment here.

Most of us today are looking for ways to live longer, whether with vitamins, special diets, or other means. According to Betzalel Bassman, one of the simplest tips for longevity is to *"honor your father and mother, that you may long to endure on the land, the Lord your G-d is assigning to you."*[10] This positive commandment reminds a person to recognize and show gratitude for what others have done for him/her. We are here on this world because of our father and mother, so we should be grateful to them. They put much time and effort into our upbringing. Showing gratitude is a strategy for a long life. When was the last time you did something or contributed something for a cause or to charity to honor your parents or in their memory? We need to say thanks to our parents or whoever raised us.

Here's another important perspective about charity that I want to share with you. The world was built upon kindness; charity could also be translated as *righteousness or justice.*[11] Sharing what we have with others is not something special, but it is an honest act, and the right thing to do. There's charity with money, and then there's charity with action. Sometimes, sharing and caring for someone else is more effective than giving money to charity. These words we hope we'll remember in our lifetime, since caring for others or our families through kind words or physical help may be all what is needed when they reach out to us for assistance. Throwing a coin into a charity box every morning except on your holy days sets the tone for the rest of your day; so make sure to make it a habit. Children can be taught this habit early in life to develop the character of being givers, not just takers.

"When you are grateful—when you can see what you have, you unlock blessings to flow in your life."
SUZE ORMAN

Chapter 9

IN GOD WE TRUST

*"The guiding principle of this Nation has been, is now,
and ever shall be, 'In God We Trust.'"*
JOHN F. KENNEDY, FEB. 9, 1961

*"Our Nation's motto, 'In God We Trust,' was not chosen
lightly. It reflects a basic recognition that there is a divine
authority in the universe to which this Nation owes homage."*
RONALD REAGAN, MARCH 19, 1981

I purposely quoted two popular former presidents from both sides of the aisle so we don't deepen the divisions in our country. I just want to point out that both cited the importance of the Divine trust during their presidency. Have you noticed that the US dollar bills and coins have "In God We Trust" on them to reminds us who to trust if we need money?

In fact, I just read an article that said that on April 22, 1864, Congress approved that significant revision to our nation's coinage, adding "*In God We Trust*" to several US coins, which was more than a small change for small change. Government officials believed at that time that it would help America through a time of crisis.[12]

Like my client Beth from Chapter 2, we have to assume responsibility for our mistakes and expand or break our old patterns, clear our limiting beliefs that hold us back, clear our energy blocks, and let go of anger and resentment in order to receive an abundance of love from our family and friends and in the physical form of cash or money. What could be the spiritual root of our financial challenges? *What tasks are we supposed to fix in this world?*

Improving our own personal connection to the Spiritual Light, or the Source has been discussed for centuries. Recently, I have noticed there seems to be a proliferation everywhere of the power of spirituality, and there's heightened interest in transcending to a state of oneness with the Divine Creator.

Some of you might criticize the focus of this book on improving money flow. Like me, you may have been taught growing up that *money is the root of all evil,* or that materialism is not congruent with spirituality. I've been there, I hear you, and the themes of the evil nature of money were embedded in my subconscious as well. These negative associations actually blocked my abundance manifestations for quite a while. Of course, I don't espouse materialism as the ultimate goal for living our lives. It is wise to learn to balance our lives as well as prioritize what is most important to provide meaning to our lives. I do believe that *living your life to actualize your G-d given gifts is a prerequisite to attain a meaningful and joyful life,* and material comforts are part of the equation. However, if everything you do is dictated by money, leading to greed, lust, egotistical behavior, or the evil need for power and dominion (I know these are all subject to debate and more detailed discussions), of course I don't subscribe to that. Money has a role in actualizing our potential, just like the biblical figures Abraham, Isaac, and especially King Solomon all became wealthy, balanced their roles in life as parents and spiritual leaders. Material prosperity is totally acceptable, and you can still be a spiritual and principled human being. So, cut the bulls**t about the guilt over making tons of money, it is OK. Transcend the culture we grew up with, *embrace prosperity, and go change the world with your wealth!*

The second of the Ten Commandments, *Thou shalt not have no other G-ds but Me*, is a phrase we all can reflect upon. Idolatry is the deification of an object or force of the created reality. Nowadays, materialism is considered the modern form of idolatry. We are consumed with how to make more and more money, and who is to say what is enough? Money gives people pleasure in many forms, be it a nice steak dinner, an exotic vacation, a private concert with your favorite singer in your home, or whatever it is that provides you with what you perceive as a source of happiness. However, pause and ask, *What is my mission with money? What if I could make a difference in this world through my money?* If you are affluent, who do you think you can empower and what contributions can you give that will change your family, your community, society, or the world? If you have limitless financial resources, have you ever tried to dream of expanding the good that you can do in whatever areas you have interest in improving? If eradication of childhood diseases in Africa is your *raison d'être*, then feel free to spend your money on that noble pursuit!

G-d desired that the good in creation should be all the more sharply defined by its contrast with the rejected evil; that *human life should be an exercise in refinement,* in distinguishing between the calories of divine energy and the sludge of putrid waste in our own self and character, our environment, and our world. Indeed, the very concept of good, as we know it, would be devoid of all meaning were it not for the challenge of rejecting the evil that vies for validation and indulgence. The ultimate pleasure lies in the experience of union with G-d through the fulfillment of His will, where pleasure resides in its most pristine, unprocessed form. The capacity of things to give pleasure is an existential paradox. *G-d desired that we be confronted with a* free choice *between good and evil so that our deeds should be meaningful and significant.*[13]

Now that I have desensitized you from the evils of being abundant, let me share with you one of the simple ways to awaken your subconscious mind and reprogram it. I know some people do not subscribe to affirmations, but many people who practice them, myself included, have made profound shifts in our belief patterns. Some people question the effectiveness of affirmations, but again, remember that we are all unique, so I welcome you to try them for yourself.

Here are a few to start with. Repeat these 10 to 15 times a day. I encourage you to remember *ABC,* which means "Always

Be Connected," by connecting first to the Spiritual Light or Divine Goodness or whatever your term is before reciting these affirmations.

> *I am connected to G- d for His abundant blessings.*
> *I will receive abundance from the Source of everything.*
> *That Spiritual light is helping me clear my financial*
> *challenges in the easiest and sweetest way.*

For those unfamiliar with the term, an affirmation statement is a statement to help shift our consciousness—primarily our subconscious, which generates approximately 95% of our thoughts. As our thoughts create our reality, these statements help shift our consciousness. Healing and shifting consciousness is both a multifaceted and incremental process.[14] Try to use these steps regularly and see for yourself. Again, journal any changes you notice.

Some millennials call this "brain hacking," but whatever is your preferred term, make attempts to practice affirmations daily with all your heart, and observe the flow of money coming your way. First notice the small discounts you may receive at grocery stores or when you are shoe shopping. Jot them down so you can monitor your progress and include your feelings, the joy you felt when you received them. It is a lot of fun, so don't ignore this tip I'm giving you.

"You open your hand and satisfy the desire of every living thing. The Lord is righteous in all His ways, and benevolent in all His deeds."

PSALMS 145: 16- 17

Chapter 10

VALUE YOURSELF

"You yourself, as much as anybody in the entire universe, deserve your love and affection."
BUDDHA

Life is not about winning, competing, or being better, smarter, or richer than our neighbor or our friend. Growing up, most of us were programmed to compete, to be the best in class. In our Asian community, we see this all the time. Just see what is posted on Facebook by people whose son graduated from Harvard with honors or whose daughter graduated cum laude from another university. Outside approval is so important in our culture that we become very competitive, from the dress we wear, to the houses we build, to the cars we drive. All these outside trimmings make people feel insecure, especially if we cannot keep up with society's definition of success and the prerequisites for happiness. Everywhere around us, we see validation that we're never good enough. If our children only got 95% in school, most parents ask, "How come you did not get 100 percent?"

"I grew up thinking that I would never, ever please my parents," recalls novelist Amy Tan. "It's a horrible feeling."

We Filipinos take pride in our academic achievements, our children's excellence in school, and anything that builds our ego. But how many times have we damaged our children or their self-esteem by comparing them to the number one in the class? Growing up, I felt insecure when I had to compete in a declamation contest. My friend Susan excelled in this, no question. She had a photographic memory and a natural ability to speak in front of hundreds of people; she could keep her composure. We were 14 years old, and she already had that knack to speak in public confidently; she became a well-respected lawyer in our city. Not me! I was freaking out deep inside, but I was programmed to compete, and of course I wanted to please my parents. I would not be surprised if that experience caused insecurity on my part when I lost in that battle. I had to delete that old pattern of failure.

In retrospect, I wished I had learned tools and strategies to just let go of that feeling of being a loser. We've heard of the famous story of Jack Ma of Alibaba being rejected by Harvard several times and still persisting in creating the Amazon of Asia—just like the original, but even bigger! I'm sure he had his secret sauce. We'd like to have some—wouldn't you?

Kristin Neff, Associate Professor of Human Development at the University of Texas and a pioneer of research on self-compassion, believes that our society's emphasis on achievement and self-esteem lies at the heart of much unnecessary and even counter- productive suffering.[15] From an early age, we are taught to build our self-esteem by competing successfully, yet competition is a losing battle. *Self-love and acceptance, balance and harmony are a big part of how we can live our lives to be happier and more abundant.*

The biggest struggle in life is the struggle to know, embrace, and accept ourselves, with all of our faults and imperfections. Many of us were raised by parents who were themselves victims. They were not taught to see their own worth, and were not really seen by their own parents. I try not to dwell on my parents' imperfections. They went through personal and financial challenges, like the Great Depression and World War II. The focus was on survival—having food on the table and minimizing the damage—rather than on love, appreciation, and intimacy. My father lucked out by being late by five minutes to his assembly at the University of Santo Tomas, otherwise he would have been another casualty of the Bataan Death March in the Philippines.[16] My mother had her own survival stories during World War II where the battle was intense, until Gen. Douglas McArthur reached Leyte shores and famously said, "I shall return." In fact, my grandmother's brother, the late Bernardo Torres Sr. was a part of this history as the governor of Leyte province at that time[17].

In this current era, individuals and families face the challenges of longer working hours and global economic uncertainty. These stresses can beat us down, or make us build walls around ourselves that are so dense that even our dearest friends, partners, spouses, and children can't get in. Yet, there is another way.

When we have the courage to let the walls down—to know and embrace ourselves, despite our human failings, we also open the door to connecting in a more caring, empathic, intimate way with the ones we love and with all living beings. Our brains are wired for survival, but also for compassion. The Dalai Lama's mantra is not in vain. When we see others are in pain, we have neurons that will remind us. Did you ever notice that during the typhoon Haiyan (Yolanda) crisis in the Philippines, donations poured in when television stations started showing pictures of dead bodies on the streets and people who seemed dazed looking for their loved ones? Our hearts always bleed for all these natural disasters. Most of us want to help.

But how about ourselves? *Are we compassionate about our own needs?* Do we listen to our soul's whisper when we feel the need to take care of ourselves? Do we follow the path where we should be going, or are we following the herd mentality? We cannot connect to our *inner self* if we are busy pleasing society. Do we create our own world and allow our own realities to anchor us? As my clients have experienced, when a family member calls for money assistance, we drop everything to help them—but meanwhile, we in the Filipino diaspora are probably deep in debt or cannot take care of our own financial obligations. It is true, it may just be $200, but that amount multiplied by three times a year adds up and could kill your budget. (Or if you're a budding Imelda Marcos, it could keep you from buying another pair of shoes. I'm just kidding! Though shopping is self-love, too.).

A former colleague told me that a relative texts her whenever an unexpected expense comes up, never even considering that my colleague has her own budget to stick to. If my colleague declines to help, she won't hear from this family member for quite a while. They have a way of literally keeping us hostage!

What happens when situations spin out of control and we encounter family dramas over finances? Sometimes, we lose our own self-esteem and feel like a victim of our own circumstances. Self-respect is too important to ignore. We have to feed our body and our soul. So, we have to let go of our old crap and truly value ourselves! We have to forgive. We find ways to let go of the lack of self-love and replace that with lots of *love for ourselves*. There are many ways to do that and as I've mentioned there are superficial ones as well as deeper ways to let go. For starters, tell yourself you are already awesome sauce. What type? Your choice, sweet and sour, hot and spicy, or whatever appeals to you!

One of the ways to take care of ourselves is prioritizing our needs instead of others all the time. Clients tell me that after they learned self-care, they realized that their children or spouses can actually take care of themselves, too, but my clients just hadn't allowed their family members to be independent. We all need to make adjustments and not judge or be too critical of ourselves. Some people can't maximize their potential because they are crippled by criticisms of their own talent. Feelings of inadequacy are so common. It happens to many, myself included.

We cannot respect and treat one another properly unless we respect and care about ourselves. Only then can we truly care about ourselves; we recognize that we were created for a reason. Let us learn to love ourselves so that we can be more open and compassionate toward others, and so that we can take down the walls that limit who we can be and what we can contribute to this world.

Just plain building our own self-esteem has its pitfalls. The best way is to have compassion for ourselves and not compete with others, and that is not easy in our Filipino diaspora culture and even back home in the country. Our close family ties have their advantages, but unfortunately drawbacks as well, and it requires discipline and tons of self-love to manage. Self-compassion is at the heart of empowerment, learning, and inner strength.

Friends, here are a few ways to self-compassion. Put them as notes on your smart phone.

Self-compassion mantras to recite daily:

What would it take for me to value myself and my contributions to the world?

What would it take for me to embrace my beauty, brilliance, and self-love?

What would it take for me to be the light and follow the path of a life of joy and abundance?

"Self-care is never a selfish act—it is simply good stewardship of the only gift I have, the gift I was put on earth to offer to others."
PARKER PALMER

Chapter 11

ENVISION YOUR FUTURE

Vision Board

Congratulations, you've read this far! Now you get rewarded with your dreams coming true. Wouldn't that be great?! Well, we are creator beings in a body, and we can increase our chances of things materializing in our lives if we focus on what we want to happen. How about if you could *shazam* prosperity into your life? What will you do if someone gives you an unexpected gift of $2 million tomorrow? Will you freak out and not know what to do? I hope not, because the process of *envisioning* is one of the ways that will bring you prosperity.

Imagine for a moment that you have an orange in your hand, you're peeling the orange, and you can feel the rind in your hands and smell the aroma wafting in the air. Notice the way your saliva is starting to accumulate around your tongue because that thought triggered your salivary glands, and now you can taste the orange. Well, we have to do the same for our financial goals. We can use the power of visualization to bring prosperity to fruition.

OK, this time, envision two million dollars were handed to you. How do you feel? Are you nervous or ecstatic? Are they in hundred-dollar bills? Do you have a vision board where you can check off the priorities in your life and where to spend that money? If you don't have one, I encourage you to create your vision board NOW and invite abundance to your path.

- Will you hug the person who delivered you this gift, or cry in disbelief?
- Will you deposit cash in the bank immediately, invest in mutual funds or get bonds as investments. How about life insurance for you and your family?
- Do you have a financial planner you'd like to talk with before making any of these decisions?
- Who will you share this bounty with? Your family, friends, community?
- Will you build a house? Where, how many rooms, how big, will it have a pool?
- If you are interested in traveling, where will you go? Backpack in Nepal or would you rather shop in Hong Kong 'til you drop?
- What impact do you want to achieve with your money: college scholarships at your local high school, or eradicate childhood diseases in your community?

Drop me a line at Familyabundancecoach.com *if you would like me to guide you through your own visualization. We can spend a few minutes reviewing your own dreams and putting together one that matches your goals in life.*

You may think this is ridiculous, but I am sure you've heard that people have done this many times. I was taking a break from writing, and when I turned on the television, Steve Harvey of NBC gave out travel gifts to people on his daytime show. He mentioned that when he was young, his mother would buy him a travel magazine that cost about $2.50, which his father found ridiculously expensive at the time, but his mother insisted on buying it for him. Mr. Harvey was in tears when he related that he would read it cover to cover and imagine where he could be until he got the next issue the following month. Well, he can afford to travel anywhere now with his success as a television host. Oprah Winfrey, Ellen DeGeneres, and many other millionaires have implemented this secret strategy to wealth manifestation. I have my own version. When I envisioned traveling to a certain country, I visualize the place, place a picture on our refrigerator, and magic happens, most of the time.

Wealth Awareness and the Numbers Game

I don't know if you can relate to this, but in college, my mother asked me to keep a strict accounting of my monthly allowance. Snacks of fried bananas on a stick were outside my budget. I managed to have them occasionally, and also brought my college buddies to Greenwich Pizza. How? Thankfully, I was assigned to go to the bank and obtain the remittance from my brother, who was a seaman, so I would get extra pesos when the dollar exchange was high (this taught me dollar exchange rates, banking etc.), Otherwise, there was no room for extra expenses. I refrained from participating in extracurricular activities because I didn't have room for error in my budget. The cost to photocopy my diploma and other papers to immigrate to the US (oh, Millennials and Generation X, you may not be able to relate since this was pre- emails and scans!) was strictly monitored; I had great command of my numbers because I had to report them to my mother.

Again, this is not a finance book, but consider this a friendly reminder for us to do a similar accounting of our income and expenses. Check how much your *net* income is and how much you are spending monthly, including cappuccinos or lattes at Starbucks, because a few dollars here and there could add up. How about potlucks at home instead of going out to dinner with friends? Someone I know who won a few million dollars in lottery still does her own manicure and pedicure. How about using Lyft or renting a car for a day instead of owning two cars you don't use daily? In Florida, many activities are free such as public parks where you can have family picnics. The Perez Art Museum, Fairchild Tropical Gardens and New World Symphonies have days that are open to the public; just check out their websites. Do you save 10% monthly or is the 10% for your family in the Philippines?

The above self-assessment is an exercise for our minds to evaluate if we have room to continue helping someone back home or whether it's time for us to stop the financial largess. Oh, by the way, there are many other ways to manifest life-changing experiences, such as pet- or house-sitting for millionaires; you get to see different parts of the world for less than you think. We'll get to that when we have a chance to chat.

How many ways can you increase your monthly income? Get into the details of any action steps you can carry out. Maybe call credit card companies to consolidate debt, or, better yet, pay cash for your purchases. Abundance is multifaceted, we can also discuss abundance in terms of relationships and finances, as a topic, are broad, but the intention is to have goals that are actionable. Businesses have plans and strategies, and so should our families, both here and in the Philippines.

In my family, our student scholars were held accountable. Sometimes, someone in our family would actually pay the tuition to the school and monitor expenses so that the student wouldn't take the financial aid for granted. Too often, I've heard of family squabbles because students did not finish school, or squandered the money sent to them. They were inconsiderate of the efforts of the OFWs, which subsequently caused a lot of anger and frustration on the ones who were working abroad. I am cognizant of the thousands of success stories that have brought prosperity to many Filipino families. Several have collectively assisted relatives who then became the source of prosperity and educated their brothers or sisters in turn.

I was an avid fan of reading finance books and magazines as soon as I arrived in America. I was fascinated with the world of money and the so-called American dream; in fact, two financial advisers have asked me to join their team (that was great for my ego!). But let's be frank about it, financial literacy is a must for everyone, and must be updated with the times. Tim Ferriss's book *The 4 Hour Work Week* is a great gift for your student scholars[18] To me personally, a college degree is no longer a prerequisite to living a life you want, but I don't want to confuse you at this time. We'll reserve this for our one-on-one discussions.

I got my early financial education from my parents and my oldest brother. Want to know how my bro really became my financial mentor? Shh ... I bounced my first check to him and really got chewed up! That taught me a big lesson, so I perused Suze Orman's books, read *Money* and *Kiplinger* magazines, subscribed to *The Wall Street Journal* and *The Economist,* and watched public television on finance topics. I paid for newsletters from *Motley Fools* and *Stansberry Research*. Two of my favorite finance gurus are Steve Sjugerrud, with his *True Wealth* and *True Wealth China Opportunities*, and Doc David Eifrig, a physician and former Goldman Sachs trader with his folksy but practical ways of trading options (not the ones you'll lose your shirt on) through his *Retirement Trader* newsletter that I signed up for when I had a yen to learn more about options and the stock market. (I get no royalties on any of the above, just mentioning my personal choices).

Notice I said *paid* because we need to understand that we have to PAY for services; we can also manifest freebies on occasion, of course. In America, as the saying goes, "you get what you pay for." This is a mentality that most of us have to adjust and get used to; some are still stuck in barter mentality and are hesitant to pay for the expertise of professional services such as financial planners or even to pay for books that can guide us on financial planning.

As you can tell, there's so much to discuss about finances. But here's my two cents on this topic: We have to be strong in our conviction to excel in whatever we do, be it in our work or in embodying financial abundance. We can lead our country out of oblivion and mediocrity. We can move mountains; if we have the will, there is a way. We can lead the Philippines out of poverty and towards prosperity one person at a time.

I'm not discounting many Filipinos who are successful professionals, entrepreneurs, or employees and who are financially stable and making a difference in uplifting the Philippine economy. We can't empower everyone, but we can assist someone to be financially independent by their own volition and NOT by coercion. Immigrants to the Philippines like Koreans, Chinese, and Israelis have prospered in our country. Like most people, we Filipinos are not just brawns for cheap labor abroad; we also have brains, and we can blaze new trails wherever we are. Gradually, we can decrease the pattern of financial co-dependency in our country.

Enhance Your System of Living

> *"You cannot add more minutes to the day, but you can utilize each one to the fullest. Before the day begins, you are not yet engaged in any physical activities. And it is only physically that you are constrained by the limits of time and place; mentally, there are no such boundaries."*
> MENACHEM MENDEL SCHNEERSON, OBM

Apple constantly upgrades the iPhone for many reasons, be it for business, functionality, to cater to consumer's needs and changing lifestyle, or myriad other purposes. My latest iPhone 7 + has great features that I love, but as with any new toy, I miss the familiarity of my iPhone 6. Still, I needed to upgrade it to match with my current communication needs. Car manufacturers do the same, not just because they want to incorporate the latest gadgets and show off sleeker versions, but mostly to enhance the driving experience of consumers and improve their business prospects. So, when was the last time you upgraded your system of living? *HUH? What do you mean?* I can hear many of you asking what this is all about.

In my teens, I loved reading books and magazines. I bought the first at the National Bookstore near Far Eastern University in Manila, where I attended nursing school. It was a personal growth book. I paid less than ten Philippine pesos from my meager allowance, which was a lot. It is still one of my favorite subjects to read because I learn so much from other people. I like to devour any wisdom they can share or interesting tips and tools to achieve my quests to live a joyful and meaningful life and make use of the divinely created unique talents gifted to us. I learned to modify my beliefs about abundance and financial scarcity. How about if you reverse scarcity phrases and see if it changes the way you perceive abundance?

There is plenty of money in the universe.
It is easy to make money.
Money loves me and money will come to me quickly.

Whatever your current financial status is, there is always room to improve it. We are shackled to the many beliefs, systems, or cultures that we grew up with and that limited our concepts of love, relationships, families, faith, and success. They are mostly based on outdated systems: the relationships we had with our families, a culture of pleasing others or what we call the "social self," keeping up with the Joneses on the block, as well as the emotional pain and experiences we had during childhood and teenage years. Let us transcend from past ways of living and incorporate ways that can enhance the many facets of our lives.

The 7 Aspects of Our Lives and Simple Strategies to Enhance Them

I. Health and Fitness

Defy aging. Create a vision for how you want to look, feel, and be in the future. What are your favorite ways to keep healthy, trim, and in shape? Have you tried yoga, Zumba, kickboxing, or a kettlebell exercise regimen? If you want to be the next champion tango dancer in Argentina, go ahead, learn it. Some swear by the amount of calories they expend, others by their efficiency. Whatever it is that enhances your health, it's up to each of us to decipher what works.

II. Personal Life and Relationships

Relationships with significant others, families, children, and parents determine your happiness in a major way. Hence they need to be enhanced, too. Pay great attention to your relationships—time is of essence here, because, sooner or later, your children grow up and oops, they don't want to be around you anymore.

Create a ritual that will upgrade your relationships. We observe the Sabbath from Friday evening to Saturday evening, so Friday night sets up our day of rest. If we go to community Sabbath dinners, we know we will have a great time with friends and other families. It starts with blessings of the wine, then homemade challah bread. *Mmmm*, the aroma of the bread alone makes me smile already.

Suggested strategies:

- Family Fun Day—Sunday brunch or Thursday night dinner or whatever that day is, *honor and respect* it. Enforce it strictly so that there are no excuses. Secondly, when you have a rough week at work, this is a day that you can look forward to, so your misery is short-lived and you will not feel like the days are long. Make it weekly if possible. A backyard barbecue with a nice organic calamansi *(Philippine lemon)* juice drink as your refresher is simple and relieves homesickness.
- Date night with your spouse/ partner, or family movie night at home with some popcorn. What's Netflix for?
- Family board game night—Have everyone bring their own dish or do a potluck if you invite neighbors or friends.

People on their deathbed don't say. "*I wish I had spent more time in the office.*" Most will say, "*I wish I had more time with my family and friends.*"

III. Character and Spirituality

I once was at a sushi bistro, and my conversation with an elderly Filipino couple made me lament of the widening communication gap between those left in the Philippines and OFWs abroad. They were in their 70s and were hesitant to visit relatives in the Philippines due to financial demands and expectations back home. I thought that there has to be a way for us to meet halfway, use love, compassion and understanding so we can all truly embrace each other. According to Rabbi Simon Jacobson, "Our actions truly matter, people matter and everything we do is important. Many of us are plain complacent, especially in this climate of cynicism and selfishness. The pressures of society have convinced us that any one person hardly matters—that we will live and die and, ultimately, the world will remain unchanged, but that attitude is simply wrong.[19]" We have to bridge this gap and I aim to start NOW.

Many books have impacted me personally and professionally. Knowledge gained from these books helped me bend my reality, question some of the rules in which I was indoctrinated, transcend the culture I grew up with, forge my own path to a life of bliss and happiness, and gave me laser-sharp focus on how I can help push humanity forward so I can make a greater impact on the world I live in. I've prepared a list for you, so I hope you check them out; I'm very confident the books will become classics in your household.

As if you don't have enough lists ... would you mind if I give you one more that will enhance your personal life. Any priorities?

- Face fears
- Love yourself
- Believe in yourself
- Seek wisdom
- Refine your goals
- Practice compassion

"Love is the transcendence of the soul over the body."
THE REBBE

IV. Social Life

They say you are the sum of the five friends you are closest to. Are you? Are you the nerdy type, techie, intellectual or offbeat? What are your hobbies? Do you like biking, reading or hiking? When was the last time you spent a day to improve your social life? Get out of your couch, get off the computer, and spend a day just taking care of this aspect of your life, since we are all interconnected and you need to breathe in fresh air. Promise to put this social life upgrade on your calendar.

1. First, check your grumpy, moody persona. If you are that type, change to an upbeat bubbly persona just for the fun of it. Can you do it? Just try, come on, I know it isn't easy. I know you fear rejection, *be aware that no one sh*its roses!*

2. Keep old friends, but make an active effort to meet new ones. How about joining a biking group in your community? We were once members of an aquarium

society (we had 10 aquariums in our living room, kitchen, and garage!), and we travelled to places with this group and were amazed by the enthusiasm and camaraderie. There were many professionals who behaved like kids and never once mentioned their work when they showed off their prized fish or the new breeds they got from the jungles of Brazil and Peru. We shopped at Mongkok Street in Hong Kong for those colorful, peaceful discus fishes that almost got us in trouble with the authorities, but it was an experience we never forgot.

3. To expand your social life, hobbies are great ways to start. If you are single, get another friend to come with you. Don't just settle for going out to overpriced, overhyped, meet-and-greet places. If you love reading, just bring your book to your favorite café and, every now and then, look up and make eye contact with people. I've personally witnessed people making connections at cafes and are now a couple.

V. Community Life and the World

We all have what it takes to champion any endeavor dear to our heart. It is a matter of how, when, where, and why we prioritize that cause that means so much to us. It makes no difference whether we saved one child out of poverty in the Philippines or saved hundreds of starving kids at Mother Teresa's orphanage in India. Just do it and do it NOW! What are you waiting for? My former student scholar niece backpacked to Nepal, volunteered to build schoolhouses, and met new friends during this adventure of a lifetime. When is your turn? Interested? Be in awe of her spectacular pictures at thoughtsofalostsole.blogspot.com or her Instagram handle @pitrocker19. You, too, might get inspired to find your new niche in life. And have lots of fun!

VI. Emotional Life

Our brains are like computers that store all our files, and our mind will access those information folders that contain similar experiences. Mine in particular loved to refresh back to painful memories that just lodged longer in different body parts: my stomach, my heart, and my psyche. Oh, sure, you know about those psychosomatic illnesses we've all heard about; we tend to remember experiences depending on the emotions we've been through. If your initial thought was negative, then you will end up feeling bad. In order to change your emotions, you can use a reminder that can help you access the right folder of positive emotions in your brain.

What are your positive triggers? Is it listening to music, or starting the day with your favorite spiritual passages or prayers? *Meditation,* anyone? Avoiding the wrong triggers is one of the most effective ways that impacted me personally, what about you? Have you ever asked yourself, *"What will it take to make me happy?* According to Martha Beck, the concept of framing our desires without trying to control other people's behavior is difficult for many people to "get."[20] Try the simple exercise below and jot down your responses.

1. Think about a situation that makes you feel angry, sad or scared. What is it about this situation that you wish were so different?
2. Think about a situation that makes you happy. What elements of the situation do you want to keep?
3. What do you want most right now?
4. What do you *really* want most right now?

VII. Intellectual and Creative Life

Educate yourself, either through audio books, written books, magazines, learning from mentors, life coaches, healers, or spiritual advisers such as priests, rabbis, and elders. Make a point of attending a lecture on subjects that you are not familiar with or that you are curious about. If you are not a gardener, attend a lecture series on different fauna and flora of your local state. Many free lectures are offered especially in public libraries or public television stations. There are online courses offered by several universities; check them out at www.coursera.org or Khan Academy for your young ones. Several states have different college scholarships, you just have to be resourceful. How about classes on painting, dancing, and organic gardening? I tried to play piano, hoping to be the next Filipino piano prodigy like *Cecile Buencamino Licad,* but no, I have to admit, I didn't have the genes. But it satisfied my curiosity. One thing off my bucket list! Some friends tried ballroom dancing and ballet, so get out of your comfort zone, it's perfectly fine.

"At every stage of your journey there will be obstacles which, however unpleasant they may seem, have the positive effect of helping you grow. Look at obstacles as transformational tools. Remember that there are no shortcuts—and that every stage is crucial to your soul's journey."
CHAIM MILLER

Bonus

More ways to be joyful and abundant whatever the amount in your bank account is right now. You don't need to decide anything, *just keep your cool and take in a few good deep breaths.*

- **Practice gratitude daily**—Make a habit of appreciating what the universe has provided you. Be fully conscious in the *now* of the creations around us that the Source has given us with no extra effort on our part to do anything. Jot down seven things for which you are grateful in your life: the bright sun, the beautiful moon, the presence of a loved one, the lunch you just had, the wind blowing on your face....

- **Forgive**—This is a trainable skill, but unfortunately, it is one of the most difficult tasks to undertake. *This is the area where most clients fail.* They *think* they have forgiven, but it was just a thought in their mind. The act of forgiving takes not just introspection and detachment from one's ego. New models of reality have to be incorporated, such as turning off the meaning-making machine. We Filipinos keep our grudges; we smile at everybody, but deep inside we are boiling with resentment and harboring grudges. When you become angry, you have lost your faith. If you really believed that what happened to you was G-d's doing, you would not have become angry at all. *"Whoever becomes angry is as if he worships idols." (Zohar1, 27b)*. Rabbi Chaim Miller quoted Rabbi Isaac Luria, considered the father of contemporary Kabbalah, saying that *"when you become angry, your soul actually departs from your body and is replaced by a substitute external soul."*[21] Forgive yourself first, then start forgiving one person at a time … and then, one event at a time.

- **Give**—Make a list of what you have that you can share with others. Most of us think it is only money that we *should* give, but what about time, love, understanding, compassion, ideas, wisdom, energy, and physical help? For Filipino students who are recipients of financial aid from OFWs, start giving of yourself by volunteering with *Gawad Kalinga* Community Development Foundation, translated in English as *Give Care,* a Philippine poverty alleviation and nation-building movement (www.gk1world.com). One of their popular projects is the GK Enchanted Farm that raises social entrepreneurs and helps local farmers create wealth in the countryside. For relatives or friends back home, you can surprise your hard-working OFW *balikbayan families* by bringing them delicacies or fruits in season; show them that you truly welcome their presence.

- **Share**—Your meager bounty. Even boiled bananas or sweet potatoes when you are going to the beach for family reunions will be appreciated. Give something back, however minuscule the contribution is. Or you can volunteer to help with aftercare; it will be much appreciated. And you will feel good that you contributed! I encourage *Balikbayans* to participate in *Balik Turo* (teach back) or OFWs to sponsor a simple lunch of salad and pizza to high school seniors and share their knowledge, experiences and success stories when they come home for vacation so these students can have a glimpse of future careers. Help develop and build confidence and be their role models! During family reunions, encourage or reward students' resourcefulness by sponsoring creative business or tourism essay writing contest so they can envision their future and give guidance on how they can achieve their dreams. (We did this at one of our family reunions and everyone had a blast, besides the students having great ideas, they felt empowered!). Together we can gradually attain income equality and become a more cohesive and productive nation.

Chapter 12

OOPS—HOLD ON TIGHT! THERE ARE OBSTACLES ON THIS JOURNEY

I*s it time to prioritize family members back home, or ourselves?* The fact that you have to think about whose needs to put at the top of your list could create major challenges in your life, especially in your financial decision-making. A friend, Ghie Camero, who has successfully educated her children in the best schools to become well-paid professionals in America, reminded me that "parents have the responsibility to educate their children and children, likewise, should reciprocate to take care of parents when they grow old and frail. Education of other relatives outside of your main family is voluntary."

You envisioned your life differently, but instead you are stuck working double shifts or working two jobs to meet all your financial obligations and assist families back home. You feel exhausted and weakened, and any comments or criticisms from family when you discuss money matters or consider cutting off the financial assistance cripple you. You are still in the martyr role, the savior in the family, the unsung hero, determined to help everyone, because in the words of clients and former colleagues, "*they just can't live without my help, they are incapable of standing on their own two feet.*"

You want family members to learn how to manage their money but there seems to always be an emergency that requires your assistance. You tried talking to them, even threatening to stop the assistance, and yet you can't decide what to do, or you just love the accolades they shower you when you go home as a *balikbayan*.

Healing Your Subconscious Body

If you have been hurt in the past because of family money matters, you have to dig deep into the subconscious mind or deeper layers of your nervous system to get them out into the open. As a nurse, you know that millions of memories and billions of bits are stored in your brain every minute, but you can choose to take gentle action and use specific techniques to change the trajectory of how you imprinted your experiences. It will take some time and the guidance of a coach to navigate you out of your comfort zone.

There are times when your internal compass will tell you to resist social pressure or to stop someone else from doing damage to you. But as long as other people aren't being dangerous or harmful, *stop worrying about what they're doing and focus on finding your own way.* You cannot control anyone else's journey through life. Focus on your own. Compassion, honesty, self-scrutiny, and an open mind are ways to interact sanely and successfully with others.

Some people claim they are too busy, don't have the time to learn the strategies, or that they don't have the money. How often do we purchase something that we use for a few times and then throw it away? How about investing time and money in ourselves? You can decrease 30 minutes from Facebook or gossip time to have plenty of time for things that matter. It is our thought process that blocks us from what we truly want to achieve in life. *Doing the same things we have been doing over and over yet expecting a different outcome sadly doesn't solve the dilemma that you are going through in your family-money drama.* Ever heard of '*Einstein time?*' You may need a coach to guide you to understand this concept.

According to a study published in the journal, *Psychology and Aging*, wisdom really does come with time.[22] Older people's brains are slow, but experience and knowledge make up for it, helping them make better financial decisions. Children are born with high levels of 'fluid intelligence," which makes them compulsively curious and great at acquiring new skills. As we age, we store an ever-increasing amount of 'crystallized intelligence," or fixed information that enables us to function effectively in situations we've seen before. A series of economic tests found the older group of study participants exhibited greater patience and better financial and debt understanding, including financial literacy. As they say, *you can get fresh, clean drinking water from a spring that has been running for a thousand years.* People who continue to confront unfamiliar situations and learn new things maintain higher levels of fluid intelligence, while their crystallized intelligence base also continues to grow.[23]

Our fear of rejection and criticism from our families hinders us, and we find it much easier to just continue what we have been doing in the past. We are familiar with the saying *you can't change others but you can only change yourself,* yet the truth is that we expect people to change for us instead of looking inside ourselves. Change is uncomfortable, I know … I was there. We are wired to fear the unknown, even when we want to change. Our brain reminds us to stop the process of changing because we are all creatures of habit. I've seen this in the hospital as a nurse practitioner: diabetic patients have difficulty reducing their ice cream intake at home despite the instructions, support, and education they received. (If I had to do it over again, I would apply the strategies I practice, but that's for the next book!)

Let us remind ourselves that the first step in the change process is the *acknowledgment that we need to change.* When potential clients call me, I give them my due respect and offer them congratulations since they crossed that bridge of recognizing that the problem exists and they want to change. Change is a multi-stage process that many behavior- change experts point to as the Trans theoretical Model of Change, or TTM. We would love to *Just Do It,* as Nike has trademarked, so we can avoid the pointless dilly-dallying that we often find ourselves doing. But, as the psychologist James Prochaska, PhD has illuminated for us, "lasting change rarely occurs as the result of a single, ongoing decision to act. Change evolves from a subtle, complex, and sometimes circuitous progression that involves thinking, hesitating, stepping forward, stumbling backward, and quite possibly, starting all over again."[24]

The TTM model proceeds through six stages: **Pre-contemplation**, **Contemplation**, **Preparation and Action**. That's only the beginning, and we can easily coast right back into preparation or contemplation if we lose our nerve, focus or steam. For our behavior change to prove sustainable, it must enter a **Maintenance** phase until it finally becomes ingrained as a stable habit. This final ongoing phase is known as **Termination** which implies that the change is now *a permanent part of our lifestyle.*

This is why the *Just Do It* model is prone to failure, because the process of change is very challenging.[25] Just check out the volume of membership at the gym in January for the people who made New Year's resolutions and compare it to March, when you have no problem getting onto your favorite treadmill machine because half of the new members have evaporated. Change involves self-awareness, dedication, resolve, and the support of a community of like-minded people. If someone wants to quit smoking, you want that person not to be hanging out with smokers, right? Otherwise, he/ she will fall back to his smoking habit oh-so-quickly!

Most Filipino nurses and OFWs who have experienced money challenges helping their families are stuck in just thinking about it instead of just doing it. I've mentioned already in the previous chapters but they are worth repeating here: *because of our ingrained culture of the bayanihan spirit, we encounter guilt (if we stop the assistance), we want to fit in to everyone's agenda, we* satisfy our need to be loved and looked up to. Truthfully, we are generous and sincerely want to help family members.

You've probably heard from many friends or colleagues that enough is enough, or your husband has said that it is time to prioritize your immediate family or your children. Due to our beautiful traditions and cultural bonds, we have difficulty cutting the emotional ties and withdrawing financial aid from our extended family in the Philippines. Whoever the recipient, whatever the reason, it always feels like it's *not quite the right time yet*. I've heard this so often from Filipino women in America, and I wish I had a magic wand to awaken them so they, too, can have joyful and abundant lives.

How do I know? I was there for years and so do many of you. *You feel weakened and you are mired in anger, sadness, and resentment.* Old, painful emotions resurface, and occasional unpleasant verbal exchanges are just not worth the discussion, you feel you are losing your power. It just seems useless to even have a heart-to-heart talk with your family. You have many questions and one of them is, why can't they figure out their finances? *The truth is, family money dramas will happen again. It is simply a matter of when.*

Some of us reach **the contemplation stage**, when we start thinking about taking action, but are not quite ready or do not have the tools to get started. Just as we have behavioral habits, we too have thinking habits. At this stage, we have to dig deep and search for internal reasons why we want to change that are unique to each of us. We connect ourselves to our higher self, our core values, and start gathering information as to how others have empowered family members in the Philippines, and then learn from them.

We start exploring the possibilities for the path to financial independence for our relatives, while still maintaining love and respect for each other. We can **visualize** how our lives here as OFWs as in my client Beth's situation, where she can save more money for her children's college education and their future vacations together as a family. You are no longer defensive when you hear someone give you alternative ideas about how to deal with the family-money drama and you actually will be supportive of this endeavor; you're gaining the confidence to envision how it will change your own life. *(No need to work overtime or night shifts, after all, your back has been achy.)*

A small percentage will make it to the **preparation stage**. You are decisive, confident and committed in making small steps. This is the time to build confidence and troubleshoot for possible obstacles that may stand in the way. As we know, prevention is better than cure. At this point, you understand the probable ways that you can fail in this *prosperity and austerity project* that you are about to tackle for the good of yourself and your family. You've got to anticipate roadblocks, so it's advisable for you to be fully aware of this possibility. You will be more open to accept the appropriate assistance and support that will move you to the next phase, which is the **action stage**.

The action stage is when you move beyond just thinking. You have actually begun the journey to transformation. I hope more will make it to this stage. During this stage, mini-sacrifices and minute choices could actually make a difference. You've heard this so often: "How do you eat an elephant? One bite at a time." We tackle family-money dramas one at a time.

Sometimes it's helpful to get the perspective of someone who has been there and done it. *A life coach can help you navigate this crucial stage.* People in this stage benefit from the emotional and physical support of others and having people around to delight in their progress and keep them accountable. In fact, Beth's son recently admitted to Beth that he need not go to an Ivy League university if he doesn't get enough financial aid or scholarship to fund his education, he'll be content to attend a less expensive state university since he doesn't want to be in debt. On the other hand, my client Rose was able to set boundaries with her brother not to quit his job as a pilot. She cut off the emotional cord of attachment, and gradually the brother realized that his sister will not fund his new business venture. And they are on good terms: a beautiful and memorable family reunion had transpired in December, 2017!

Maintenance stage is when you have managed to stay in action mode for at least six months and have overcome the obstacles thrown at you. Stress, crisis, loss of emotional support, or other life changing events can trigger a relapse. In the cities, we listen to reports of traffic jams to update us on the road conditions. Likewise, campers and hikers report to park rangers regularly when they embark on hiking trips. Similarly, it is advisable for you to report your progress, and discuss and tweak your plans with someone who has experienced the journey, especially if you encounter stress-inducing resistance from your family.

Stay in the **maintenance stage** for a while, and you'll reach a point where you can't really imagine going back to the way it was before. You also want to celebrate milestones, and you are allowed to eat a few scoops of Magnolia ice cream to reward your efforts occasionally. Can I get a big smile, please?

I prefer to call the last stage the **empowered stage** instead of using the TTM term of *termination stage.* You have now completely integrated the behavior change in yourself, the tools and strategies you struggled to learn initially are now part of your being and consciousness; you don't even have to think what to say, or how to react when family-money challenges re-occur. You are confident of your decision, and no longer worried about what people say. Your *social-self* (the part of your psyche who is trying to please others or society) will no longer be heard whispering and yelling at you by your *essential self* (the now happy and abundant you). You will now be able to ignore criticisms and you will be an expert in listening to the voice of your *higher self. Others can no longer disrupt your joyful and abundant existence.*

When you reach this point, you will have the power within you to thrive. You will have the wisdom, strength, skills, secret tools, and will be creating the life of your dreams, experiencing unprecedented personal growth and creativity. You will be following the beat of your own drummer, the shepherd of your tribe. You will be able to focus on your own agenda and start thinking of what contributions you can impart to make this world a better place to live. Wow, what a life, it is so worth the time and effort to reach this stage!

Now, you need a helping hand to navigate you through this treacherous water of decision-making. You want to transform yourself and realign your financially co-dependent family members, you just don't know what to do. Should you do it now, or wait four years until so-and-so graduates college, or should you just continue working overtime for the extra money to send back to the Philippines?

You have a choice, but how about if you choose based on what your heart tells you and what is comfortable for you. We all have a servant's heart, we all want to help. In fact, you may have helped your family for more than *10 years. What is enough? When is enough?*

Bear in mind that the expertise of someone who has experienced similar situations is readily available when you are ready to be served. Do you know what stage you are in? Or do you need assistance to figure out where you are at this moment? Then, *kababayan*, send me a note at www.Familyabundancecoach.com and together we can decipher your family-money drama.

Conclusion

There are many good people in our country who deservedly need assistance, but many prefer to take the fruits of the labor of others. Unfortunately, we will perpetuate co-dependency if we do not start correcting this from within ourselves. *Givers fail because their idea of giving is limited to cash or money gifts.* If we can reframe the term *giving* to encompass a broader perspective, then we'll be on our way to a more progressive society made up of people who are contributing to their own bright future.

Here's how to expand our concept of giving:

- Guidance on ethics, morality, integrity, and honesty
- Financial planning and literacy to start at home and within families– If providing monetary help, set boundaries regarding amount, length of time, goals to achieve and provide caveats when financial aid could be abruptly stopped such as medical emergencies on the financier.

- Partner with parents or student scholars for a 50/50 split on educational expenses for accountability so they too can take pride that they contributed.
- Mentor high school or college graduates for entrepreneurial opportunities
- Incorporate creative ways to use resources unique to our culture
- Meet the local needs of our people such as food, agribusinesses and eco-tourism instead of imitating western businesses
- Show how to expand their minds and connect them to potential mentors. Offer a matching program if you plan to assist families in their business proposals.

Do you still ask yourself *why* are things happening to you? Why is your money faucet still leaking, or why does working a double shift either at night or daytime seem like your only way of earning extra cash to help family? Have you ever thought that there are hundreds of ways to make an extra income and there's plenty for everyone?

Where did you go wrong? Why do cars break down, and why does one expense lead to another? Why, oh, why can't your family understand your own mounting expenses where you live?

I bet you think that if you read this book cover to cover (thanks, by the way), you will magically master the flow of abundance. I bet 99 percent of you will put this book aside without taking *action*.

Instead of just wanting to change your money situation, outlook, and perspective in life, how about making the first action steps? Be bold and ask yourself, "What is my next small or big step to get new answers to my dilemma?" What if it turns out that you get better and more profound shifts by doing something different, having awareness that there is a silver lining and that it is within your capacity to change and catapult you to be a more abundant and joyful being? Then you won't have to worry if you have to educate the whole clan, better yet, why not make a *trust* to educate the whole town or city where you came from? Wouldn't that be cool? *You* have the power within you to change the things around you, but it has to start with YOU; remember that. *Omm*…. Take one more deep breath!

I did not forget the highly controversial topic ingrained in our culture, and that is hospitality. We love to accommodate friends or families as houseguests, and in many instances, some may overstay, especially if we are reciprocating *utang na loob* (debt of gratitude) or financially our *kababayan* can't afford to be on their own yet and plainly have no other place to live since they just came from the Philippines. The situation can get sticky if boundaries are not set early, if you know what I mean. We are aware of the old quote from Benjamin Franklin: "Guests, like fish, begin to smell after three days," and invasion of privacy can be an issue. See, I told you this is a complicated matter. I was not oblivious to this topic but due to space constraints, we have to end here. However, I can share with you a few tips and tools to ease this burden in the event this occurs in your family. Check out my website at www.Familybundacecoach. com and download my checklist. Promise to send me a note if the strategies worked so I can say *salamat* (thank you) back to you for reading my book. Looking forward to hear from you!

"Don't focus on things or people that cannot change…
*Instead, endeavor to **change from within yourself**.*
Enhance your system of living so that it suits you, not
others. You owe it to yourself to live a life of joy and
prosperity so you can actualize your full potential and
shine your own light in this world"
BELEN LORETO GRAND

End Notes

[1] Suze Orman, in Suze Orman: PH money culture must change. Business and Culture, Posted May 21, 2013.

[2] Dias, B.G. and Ressler, K.J in *Nature Neuroscience* http://dx.doi.org/10.1038/nn.3594 (2013)

[3] De Vera, Ben O in *OFW remittances hit record high in 2016. Inquirer.net/Business*

[4] Rajah Humabon (Ca.1521). History of Cebu: The Battle of Mactan. https://aboutphilippines.ph

[5] Baruch Emanuel Erdstein in Kabbalah: A brief Definition. www.chabad.org or Kabbalah Online

[6] Beck, Martha. Finding Your Own North Star, *Reading Your Emotional Compass*. Three Rivers Press, New York ©2001, pages 167-168.

[7] Simmons, Rabbi Shraga in *Lashon Hara or Gossip* @www.aish.com

[8] Schusterman, Chana Rachel in *The Kabbala of Self-Refinement* @ www.Chabad.org.

[9] Grabhorn, Lynn. Excuse Me Your Life Is Waiting. Hampton Roads Publishing Co. Charlotesville, VA. ©1999

[10] Gratitude and *Tzedakah* (charity). www.Chabad.org

[11] The Rebbe.org/Another Form of Charity—The Rebbe's message to an eight-year old child.

[12] Hartog, Jonathan Den. *'In God We Trust, Even At Our Most Divided'*, Wall Street Journal, April 20, 2017

[13] *The Evolution of Pleasure*. From the Teachings of the Lubavitcher Rebbe. Courtesy
Of MeaningfulLife.com

[14] Targan, Chaim David. in *The Power of Ani Ma'amin to Shift Beliefs'* www.chaimdavid.org

[15] Neff, Kristin *Self Compassion*. William Morrow © April, 2011

[16] Bataan Death March. History Channel World War II. History.com

[17]Cannon, Hamlin. LEYTE: The Return To The Philippines, Center of Military History, United States Army. Washington, DC, 1993, page 19.

[18] Ferris, Timothy. *The 4-Hour Workweek. Crown Publishers*, New York, © 2007.

[19] Jacobson, Simon. *Toward a Meaningful Life*. Perennial Currents. Harper Collins Publishers. New York, New York 10022. © 2002, page 298.

[20] Beck, Martha. Finding Your Own North Star, *Reading Your Emotional Compass*. Three Rivers Press, New York ©2001, pages 167-168.

[21] Miller, Chaim. TORAH –The Five Books of Moses in *Parsha Pinchas*, © 2011 Lifestyle Books. Brooklyn, New York, page 980.

[22] Innes, Emma, Daily Mail Science in *Wisdom really comes with age*: Older people's knowledge and experience means they make better decisions.

[23] Beck, Martha. Finding Your Own North Star in *Be Like Water Flowing*. Three Rivers Press, New York ©2001, page 363

[24] Prochaska, J.O & Proschaska, J.M. *Changing to Thrive*: overcome the top risks to lasting health and happiness. © 2016 Hazelden Publishing, Center City, MN.

[25] Sholl, Jessie. Experience Life Magazine in *Break a habit, Achieve a goal, Transform your life.* November, 2011

Recommended Reading

Code of an Extraordinary Mind, by Vishen Lakhiani

Choose Yourself, by James Altucher

Excuse Me, Your Life Is Waiting, by Lynn Grabhorn

Finding Your Own North Star, by Martha Beck

The Big Leap, by Gay Hendricks

The 9 Steps to Financial Freedom, by Suze Orman

Toward a Meaningful Life, by Simon Jacobson

Acknowledgments

My gratitude to my father, Cesar Torres Loreto (RIP), for his love and generosity.

I am forever grateful to my oldest brother, Adrian. Thank you for all your efforts and time spent in the frigid winters of Wyoming and Colorado and for your vision to uplift everyone in the family.

To my brother Cesar, for keeping the organic vegetable garden that sustained many.

Heartfelt appreciation to my sister, Anne, who accepted the mantle my mother had given her to ensure all her younger brothers and sister become professionals. I recognize your agony to leave your son and brave the cold winters of Austria and Switzerland as one of the pioneer Filipino nurses in Europe.

To my brother Joseph, who kept our fort in the Philippines while we were all away.

To my brother Prix, for allowing me to keep the extra cash during my lean college years.

To my brother Mello, the Einstein of the family, for always keeping his composure and being there for me in our frequent moves.

To my brother Ferrer, for his tremendous help in organizing our office and garage.

To all my brothers- and sisters-in law, nephews, nieces, and grandchildren. Thank you for being a part of our extended family and sharing your life and pictures on Facebook.

My gratitude to my aunt, Col. Anacorita Santa Iglesia (RIP), then chief nurse of the Armed Forces of the Philippines. It is never too late to let her know that her Vietnam war escapades and career inspired me as a young nursing student.

I am forever grateful to the Rebbe, Menachem Mendel Schneerson OBM, for the CHABAD rabbis, *rebbetzins*, especially Nechama Harlig and Chani Katz, and the Jewish thinkers and speakers who have enhanced my understanding of the relationship we have with our Divine creator as well as enriched my spiritual life. Words are not enough to express my appreciation for all your wisdom.

To the amazing, brilliant and super coach, Angela Lauria, for your selfless dedication to empower many people so they can make the contributions they were born to do in this world.

To Tamara Arnold and Maggie McReynolds for all the assistance you've given me.

To Christie Marie Sheldon, Cindy Sheldon, Jacki Whitford, and the Unlimited Abundance family; thank you for caring for us to change from within to become our authentic selves.

To Dean Felicidad Elegado (RIP) and Lydia Palaypay of the FEU—Institute of Nursing, for your leadership in the nurture and education of some of the best nurses in the world and for giving us space for personal and professional growth.

To my college buddies, Elinor Medina, Fely del Mundo, Gloria Mendoza, Lucy Letim, Luz Quirimit, Nina Magpantay, Ghie de Los Reyes Camero, Grace Lozano, Freddie Fernandez, and all my FEUIN class '80-A, nursing family for the memories and camaraderie we all shared.

To my high school classmates of BNHS class 1975, know that I treasure your friendships and cherish the experiences we all shared.

To my former roommate, Malu Vendiola Castillo; former colleagues Luz Juan, Geraldine Guiwo, Lolita Wee, Nona Macasiray, Agnes and Rudy, Helen De Guzman, Rosalyn and Elmer Cacayorin, Ramona Salinel, Leny Paguio, Nenette Mates, Maricar Albea, Cindy Cachola, Esperanza Abinsay, Evelyn Patria Sussman, and all my former colleagues at Miami General Hospital, I thank you for the emotional support that sustained us, especially when we all got homesick for our beloved Philippines.

To the many mentors and colleagues who provided me guidance in many ways, such as Dr. Eugene Schiff, Dr. George Burke III, Dr. Joshua Miller, Dr. Rajender Reddy, Dr. Jaime Merchan, Dr. Divina Grossman, Dr. Jason Radick, Anne Harlowe, Lowella Baptista, Kamara Mertz Rivera, Mary Hill, Maria de Medina, Diane Saunders, Anne Rosen, and Deborah Whippler. If I forgot to mention your names, know that I appreciated your presence in my life.

To my cousins, Kelly Loreto Cancio, Wilhelmina Loreto Kuszelewicz, Brenda Loreto, Thelma Goetz, Evelyn DeVries,

Sister Rebecca, Cher and Melvin Loreto, for adopting me as your lost cousin and the positive influences I learned from you all during my college years.

To Jian Moses Handugan for your kindness and volunteering as my Uber chauffeur.

To the Morgan James Publishing team: Special thanks to David Hancock, CEO & Founder for believing in me and my message. To my Author Relations Manager, Margo Toulouse thanks for making the process seamless and easy. Many more thanks to everyone else, but especially Jim Howard, Bethany Marshall, and Nickcole Watkins.

Many thanks to my clients and future clients. My passion and heartfelt dedication to make a *difference in your life* so you can reach your full potential and live a joyful and abundant life will guide me to be the best life coach you can have.

Most of all, I thank the Divine Creator, for sustaining me and my family; *may we always be aware of the purpose of our mission in life.*

About the Author

Belen Loreto Grand immigrated from the Philippines in 1982, and is an Advanced Registered Nurse Practitioner. She has held diverse positions at the University of Miami and Jackson Health System as research administrator, liver and GI transplant coordinator, Oncology  ARNP, and entrepreneur. She serves her clients through one-on-one coaching and group strategy sessions, providing them with tools and strategies to create a life that catapults them to achieve their limitless potential. Her heart-centered work allows clients to be their authentic self and makes room for love, peace, and prosperity both at home and at work in order to meet the needs of their families in their home country.

Belle, as she is fondly called, was inspired to be a life coach after going through her own personal and spiritual transformation. She combines her love of family and interest in improving abundance manifestation for many individuals, having assisted in the education and financial independence of many family members for more than 25 years. Her goal is to empower individuals by guiding them through a process that shifts their consciousness and limiting beliefs via goal setting and envisioning and creating inspired actions to make their life a living masterpiece.

Belle lives with her husband Robert, who has authored a children's picture book, *The Cosmic Carrot* (www.cosmiceditions. net). After typhoon Haiyan (Yolanda) hit Leyte, Philippines in 2014, she and her husband partnered with a crowdfunding platform to restore agricultural lands and improve farming techniques, resulting in the income of farmers having multiplied several times (www.globalgiving.org/17225).

Connect with me:
www.Familyabundancecoach.com
Facebook: Belen Loreto Grand

Thank You

Salamat ... Thank you!

Thanks for reading Family Matters. This is just the beginning of a life-changing and worthwhile future. I sincerely hope this book has provided you with peace of mind as you embark on the journey to empower yourself in the decision-making process.

Ready To Take The 1st Step?
Clarity is power. Get ready to become more clear about where you are, and what is possible than ever before.

Definitely, we all know we have families who deserve financial assistance back in our country. Do you want to continue helping your family and need to learn the many unconventional ways to receive abundance so you will have plenty of resources to continue the monetary help? OR, are you ready to stop helping family NOW and need guidance to maintain family harmony during this challenging process? Download a free checklist at www.Familyabundancecoach.com.

Morgan James
Speakers Group

↗ www.TheMorganJamesSpeakersGroup.com

We connect Morgan James published
authors with live and online events
and audiences who will benefit
from their expertise.

Morgan James makes all of our titles available
through the Library for All Charity Organization.

www.LibraryForAll.org